SWIVEL TO SUSTAINABILITY

A FULL SYSTEMS BUSINESS TRANSFORMATION GUIDEBOOK

BY LEYLA ACAROGLU

ILLUSTRATIONS & GRAPHICS BY EMMA SEGAL

Written by Leyla Acaroglu (PhD)
www.leylaacaroglu.com

Illustrations + design by Emma Segal
www.emmasegal.co

Editing and text contributions by
Jamie Ferrell and Emma Segal

First Published 2022
Disrupt Design

ISBN 979-8-218-05933-0

For questions or comments
hello@disruptdesign.co

Cover photographs sourced from Unsplash.com

www.swivelskills.com
www.disruptdesign.co
www.unschools.co

A NOTE FROM THE AUTHOR

Over the last 20 years of my career in sustainability and design, I've had the pleasure of working with all sorts of individuals and organizations, from Fortune 500 companies and academic institutes through to not-for-profits, entrepreneurs and community leaders.

But often I have found myself in meetings and conversations with senior leaders from different industries and been shocked by the knowledge gap around the comprehension of core terms and concepts related to sustainability.

Despite more than 30 years of progress, many workers ranging from recent graduates to seasoned experts lack the foundations on approaches to climate action, the circular economy and impact assessments (both social and environmental).

This has been a major motivator for writing this guidebook: to lay out the foundations of making change through sustainability in an accessible and actionable format.

Having founded several entrepreneurial initiatives myself, I know what it's like to rapidly upskill in a new topic that has become critical to business success. As an experiment, I checked to see what kind of information someone searching sustainability would find online and was quite alarmed by the lack of clarity, the greenwashing and the disconnect between concepts and actions.

And so, I decided to write this guidebook and to develop a new training initiative called Swivel Skills to help businesses reduce impacts, improve products and create value in the economy in sustainable and regenerative ways.

This guidebook is thus designed for the leaders, managers, workers and entrepreneurs interested in creating positive change through their daily work practices and business endeavors. It covers the basics but also dives into the actions you can take, with practical tools and prompts embedded to get you started right away.

I believe that substance-based sustainability is a pathway to regeneration. It's a complex topic, but here you'll find the key elements dissected into manageable parts so that you can use these as building blocks to create your organizational transformation.

The future is defined by our actions today. What you do matters, and what we all do collectively will help decide how positive our future is.

Leyla Acaroglu, August 2022

ABOUT THE AUTHOR
LEYLA ACAROGLU

Dr. Leyla Acaroglu is an internationally-known sustainability provocateur, sociologist and award-winning designer focused on systems thinking, sustainability sciences and creative change-making.

She was named Champion of the Earth by the United Nations, Change-Maker by Linkedin and is a mainstage TED speaker who leads presentations with leaders around the world on activating positive change for a sustainable, circular and regenerative future.

Leyla started her career in environmental impact assessment, working to advance life cycle thinking in education and product development. She developed one of the first online life cycle assessment tools for designers and has created many tools that activate science-based approaches to sustainability.

As a serial social entrepreneur, she founded The UnSchool, an experimental knowledge lab for adults, developed the Disruptive Design Method and is the CEO of Disrupt Design, a creative agency where she has developed the corporate training platform Swivel Skills.

ABOUT THE ILLUSTRATOR
EMMA SEGAL

Emma Segal is a multidisciplinary designer focused on activating sustainability through creative production. She specializes in communicating complex social and environmental concepts and designs creative change-making projects to support the growth of the circular economy at all levels.

Emma's work is deeply informed by two decades of experience designing and producing locally and internationally- manufactured consumer goods, along with formal training in international relations, design and illustration. She holds a Masters degree in changing the way designers create products, with work spanning multi-million dollar programs for multi-national organizations through to bootstrapped entrepreneurs.

Her experience offers a dynamic creative approach to challenging the status quo by design. She facilitates workshops around the world both in sustainable design and creative communication for change as a certified UnSchool Educator.

HOW THIS GUIDEBOOK WORKS

This guidebook is designed so you can flip through and access the main content in clear, easily digestible segments. You will find interactive worksheets throughout, as well as meeting and workshop topics for discussion to help you integrate sustainability into your business practices. Read from start to finish, or jump to the section that will either help you get started, make progress or motivate you to take action.

PART 1: INTRODUCTION TO SUSTAINABILITY

The term sustainability is used to describe actions that seek to **transform negative impacts into proactive, positive ones** for both the planet and for people. This includes different movements, such as the **circular economy, regenerative design** and **impact assessment**.

This section covers the foundations of what sustainability is (and what it isn't). You will gain comprehension of key terms and concepts related to the different movements and approaches, along with a holistic view of sustainability as it applies to business.

PART 2: ORGANIZATIONAL CHANGE

Taking action to address the **environmental and social impacts** of your business is not just about responding to growing market trends or ensuring that you are **operating ethically** and being a responsible company; it's also about having foresight and being **future ready** now.

This section shows how to create a proactive approach to sustainability whilst growing your business and retaining excellent workers by seeing challenges as opportunities and being willing to adapt and transform, rather than maintain the status quo. It's all about overcoming the barriers, activating change and building toward transformation.

PART 3: THE 3D SUSTAINABILITY IN BUSINESS FRAMEWORK

The 3D Framework is designed to help you **take action** and ensure that your organization is continually improving and evolving how you **design** your products, **run** your operations and **engage** with your customers and stakeholders so that **sustainability is integrated** into your organization's DNA.

This section dives into the high-level approach of the three dimensions of sustainability in business (operations, products and experiences) and includes practical tools for each dimension that will guide you in applying changes.

Sustainability is the major innovation opportunity of our time — a chance for organizations to fully embrace a sincere, full systems transformation that opens the pathway to not just sustaining our beautiful planet, but restoring and regenerating it.

This guidebook is designed to help busy professionals seize this innovation opportunity and activate full systems sustainability in any sized business. Throughout this guidebook's chapters, you will learn the foundations of sustainability, gain the tools needed to overcome barriers to organizational and cultural change and then discover the main tactical approaches that businesses can use to create a positive impact in operations, products, and experiences.

Be a part of the growing community of business leaders and professionals who are challenging the status quo of a wasteful linear economy and building the sustainable circular future that we all deserve.

No matter if you are a novice or expert in sustainability, this guidebook will help you gain the language and skills to launch or advance your leadership and drive us all into a more sustainable, equitable, circular and regenerative future.

WHO IS THIS GUIDEBOOK FOR?

This guidebook is designed for business professionals wanting to embark upon, expand or rapidly level up their sustainability transformation. It does not waste time detailing all the social and environmental issues that are perpetuated by activities in business (as you should be well aware of issues such as climate change, the global waste crisis and pollution); instead, you will find clear information, the motivations for business transformation and proactive steps to take.

No matter your industry, role or position within a small or large company, you will find valuable information to advance your green skills for you to understand, activate and create change.

WHAT WILL YOU GET OUT OF READING IT?

This guidebook is fundamentally about organizational change, as the transformation from a linear to a circular business model requires shifting mindsets, innovating beyond ways of the past and redesigning the way we work as well as the products we create.

One of the main topics we'll address is how to overcome the barriers that occur when people are confronted with the need to transform their business practices into a new, dynamic and complex way of creating value.

Throughout these pages, you will find practical tools and techniques needed to enact organizational change, along with the three-dimensional sustainability in business framework, developed to support businesses in transforming their operations, products and experiences.

Like any field of professional practice and academic theory, there are differing perspectives on sustainability. For the context of this book, written specifically for professionals working in the business world, sustainability is framed as a practical and science-based approach to rectify past and present negative impacts by using a technical framework that transforms them into positive effects.

Here you will find a toolset for the full systems transition to an environmentally and socially- safe operating space, with the specific objective of supporting a wider transformation to a restorative and regenerative future.

There is some debate about how useful sustainability is in a climate-ravaged world, which includes calls to abandon it and replace it with regenerative approaches to business. I do not see this as an "either-or" situation, but instead as an "and-then" approach.

This means that in order to get to a state of regeneration (where we give back more than we take), we need to transition through different stages of sustainability, from the low-hanging fruit of improving operational efficiency, through to developing impact-driven products and supply chains, along with considering the whole experience of customers, stakeholders and employees.

Combined, this three-dimensional approach provides a roadmap to go from the status quo of unsustainability and negative impacts to full systems sustainability, which looks to transform the way products, services and experiences are created in order to set society up for a regenerative transformation.

Sustainability as an approach, movement, technical skillset and business objective is very different from the word "sustainable", which is used in a variety of different contexts to describe something as being able to be sustained into the future.

Sustaining an unhealthy system is not the goal. Extraction, exploitation and the growth-at-all-costs mindsets are not sustainable. Nor are products that are designed to be wasted or business practices that don't take full responsibility for the entire value chain or the impacts that their activities have on the world. These are what we need to challenge.

Sustainability is not at all about sustaining the status quo — it's about integrating the concept of sustainment into the DNA of an organization and our culture at large. It's about reconfiguring society so that we understand and work within the systems that sustain life on Earth. The goal is to find ways of meeting human needs today while also advancing society for the future — but not at the expense of other living systems, the planet, or the quality of life for future generations.

With healthy ecosystems, biodiversity and nature being critical to our collective success, sustainability is the guiding principle for both sustaining and restoring the systems that support life so we can progress into a positive future.

PART 1   8

INTRODUCTION TO SUSTAINABILITY

1.1 SUSTAINABILITY IN BUSINESS   10

1.2 THE FOUNDATIONS OF SUSTAINABILITY   23

1.3 CORE SUSTAINABILITY CONCEPTS & THINKING SHIFTS   31

PART 2   68

ORGANIZATIONAL CHANGE

2.1 A FUTURE-POSITIVE APPROACH   70

2.2 CULTURES OF CHANGE   70

2.3 HUMAN NATURE AND BARRIERS TO CHANGE   73

2.4 ACTIVATING ORGANIZATIONAL CHANGE   82

2.5 TOOLS FOR ENABLING CHANGE   85

PART 3   93

THE SUSTAINABILITY IN BUSINESS 3D FRAMEWORK

3.1 THE SUSTAINABILITY IN BUSINESS 3D FRAMEWORK   95

3.2 OPERATIONAL IMPACTS   106

3.3 PRODUCT LEVEL IMPACTS   112

3.4 EXPERIENTIAL IMPACTS   126

EPILOGUE   136

ACTIVITIES & WORKSHEETS

PART 1

→ **WORKSHEET:** Past Change Identification **20**

→ **WORKSHEET:** Future Change Identification **21**

ACTIVITY: An Overview of your Sustainability Journey **22**

ACTIVITY: Reframing Sustainability at Work **27**

→ **WORKSHEET:** Benchmarking Leaders **30**

ACTIVITY: Regeneration at Work **35**

→ **WORKSHEET:** Divestment Opportunities **36**

ACTIVITY: Observing Circular Systems in Nature **39**

ACTIVITY: Assessing the Top 10 Climate Actions **45**

ACTIVITY: Considering Circular Design Around Us **50**

ACTIVITY: Considering New Ways of Thinking **54**

ACTIVITY: Systems Mapping **59**

ACTIVITY: Exploring Greenwashing **63**

→ **WORKSHEET:** Greenwashing Checklist **64**

ACTIVITY: Part 1 Reflection Recap **67**

PART 2

ACTIVITY: How Does your Organization Handle Change? **72**

ACTIVITY: How Limiting Forces Impact You **79**

ACTIVITY: Exploring the Forces that Limit Change **81**

ACTIVITY: Creating a Code of Conduct **84**

ACTIVITY: Organizational Theory of Change **89**

ACTIVITY: Part 2 Reflection Recap **92**

PART 3

ACTIVITY: Familiarize Yourself with the 3D Sustainability in Business Framework **97**

→ **WORKSHEET:** Waste Audit **109**

→ **WORKSHEET:** Life Cycle Mapping **116**

→ **WORKSHEET:** Journey Mapping **131**

→ **WORKSHEET:** Circular Redesign **134**

ACTIVITY: Part 3 Reflection Recap **135**

EPILOGUE

→ **WORKSHEET:** Action Planning **138**

→ **WORKSHEET:** Policy Checklist **140**

→ **WORKSHEET:** Goal Setting **141**

→ **WORKSHEET:** Past & Future Opportunities **142**

PART 1

INTRODUCTION TO SUSTAINABILITY

About five years ago, I was invited by a food and packaging company to speak to their senior managers and product development team of a snack-food arm of their company to open up a dialogue about sustainability.

I walked into a room filled with samples of single-use snack products and a group of people eagerly discussing what the next big trend will be. Popped popcorn in tiny Styrofoam cups and clamshell plastic packaging for cookies to prevent them from breaking were among the samples of packaged food in front of me.

As I finished my presentation, I was met with stern looks and confused reactions: "This is not what people want from us — they want convenience! ...At least some of this is recyclable, right?"

I explained the many ways that they could dematerialize, change packaging materials and offer clean and circular solutions to customers, but I left that room concerned that the priority was so geared toward profit that all my offerings were seen as a waste of time.

There was no regulation demanding that they take action, and while there was some customer demand, their products were selling. So, why change something when it's working so well?

Fast forward to today — these types of companies are being told by the major retailers that if they don't have sustainable packaging, then their items will no longer be stocked. Customers are frustrated by complex recycling systems, and the issue of ocean plastic waste has become a major global concern.

Had they been willing to pioneer change then, they would have been ahead of this trend. But instead, they stayed true to their status quo and are now scrambling to figure out a solution for their products.

1.1 SUSTAINABILITY IN BUSINESS

It starts with a mindset shift.

To embrace sustainability in business is to acknowledge that all business decisions have significant impacts on the planet and people, in both negative and positive ways.

Employment opportunities, the products you produce and the value you create are all positive contributions to society. But in the process of doing business, the emissions generated, the materials extracted, the waste created and the people contracted along the supply chain can all contribute to negative impacts on people and the planet. That's why one of the main goals of sustainability in business is to understand where impacts occur and then take sincere and significant actions to rectify them. In doing so, the value you create is not done at a deficit to the planet as a whole.

Moving through the different stages of sustainability in business decision making, it starts from a basic operational level and progresses to the products and services you buy and sell, through to the experiences your company, customers and key stakeholders have in relation to your business as a whole.

All businesses have impacts, some more significant than others, but as it stands, no matter their size or stature, many companies operate with limited or no understanding of the impacts of their actions, often resulting in negative unintended consequences to people and the planet.

To understand impacts, there are technical approaches to collecting data, assessing the broader effects they have and then taking action to alleviate and transform them (this is what we go into detail on in Part 3 of the guidebook).

The goal is for full systems sustainability to lead to restorative and regenerative outcomes.

This is one of the main objectives of starting or expanding a sustainability journey: get the information needed to know your impacts, and then make changes to your operations, product design, supply chains and stakeholder engagement to ensure that you are taking full responsibility for the negative effects and converting them into positive ones.

SUSTAINABILITY AS A BUSINESS OBJECTIVE

Sustainability is the business imperative of our time. Because customers and employees want to invest in, buy from and work for companies that have social and environmental values, it's no longer good enough to buy carbon credits and claim a product is "carbon neutral" or has recycled materials in it.

These insincere approaches do little to convince a more savvy audience that your actions are doing good as a whole company. People want to engage with products and services that are not simply doing less harm, but actually doing significant good, working toward giving back more than they have taken.

In the context of business, sustainability is about ensuring that workers, workplaces, and business structures are operating in an ethical, equitable, ecologically benign and economically viable way (whereas from a personal perspective, sustainability is more about the choices we make when consuming goods and services).

In short, it's about integrating an approach to doing business that meets the needs of customers and workers without impacting the planet at large. In order to achieve this, every person within the company needs to have basic sustainability skills, be aware and aligned with policies and commitments and be willing to adapt their approaches to meet bigger picture goals.

In the age we live in now, every job is a climate job, so we all have the opportunity to do good through our work, be it in accounting (such as ESG see page 143), HR, Design, Management, Product Development, Retail, Customer Service, Hospitality, or any of the millions of roles that make up the economy.

Sustainability offers significant untapped opportunities for creating transformative change in the way products are produced, operations are managed, supply chains are created, and stakeholders are engaged with. This takes individuals working within teams and collaborating for effective change to take hold.

FROM ADD-ON TO INTEGRAL

In the past, many organizations have fallen into the trap of thinking sustainability is an add-on or a side project for some good-intentioned team members, or that it's a simple tick-the box style activity that has to be done to meet regulations.

As a result, some have been caught greenwashing (making claims that can't be validated and misleading customers) because they didn't hire people with the right skillset or invest enough resources in doing sustainability well.

Greenwashing happens when more money is spent on marketing the green credentials of a product, service or company, rather than ensuring that it actually has positive benefits by doing the R & D, getting the scientific data to validate the claims and ensuring that the product lives up to its marketing claims. This ends up misleading consumers and perpetuating harmful environmental myths in the process (if you want to jump to more detailed information on greenwashing right now, go to page 62 for a deep dive on what to do to avoid it).

The difference between doing superficial and substance-based sustainability is in embracing

The end goal with any sustainability journey should not be to tick a box or make a green marketing claim, but to make a positive impact in all aspects of your business activities and in doing so, have a positive impact on the world at large.

the full systems transformation that is needed to ensure all aspects of your business, including the cultural aspects, have taken on this great challenge as an opportunity for change and grown through that. That's what true innovation is all about: using parameters as guidelines for new ideas and approaches to solving problems.

MINDSET SHIFTS

Can you imagine any person or business leader today who would actively say that they didn't want to help create a better, healthier future for us all? By not embracing sustainability in a significant way, this is what any leader is conveying — that they don't care about the future we are creating with our actions today.

That's why your activation of a full systems approach to sustainability in your business will put you at the forefront of your industry's response to the great disruptions of our time.

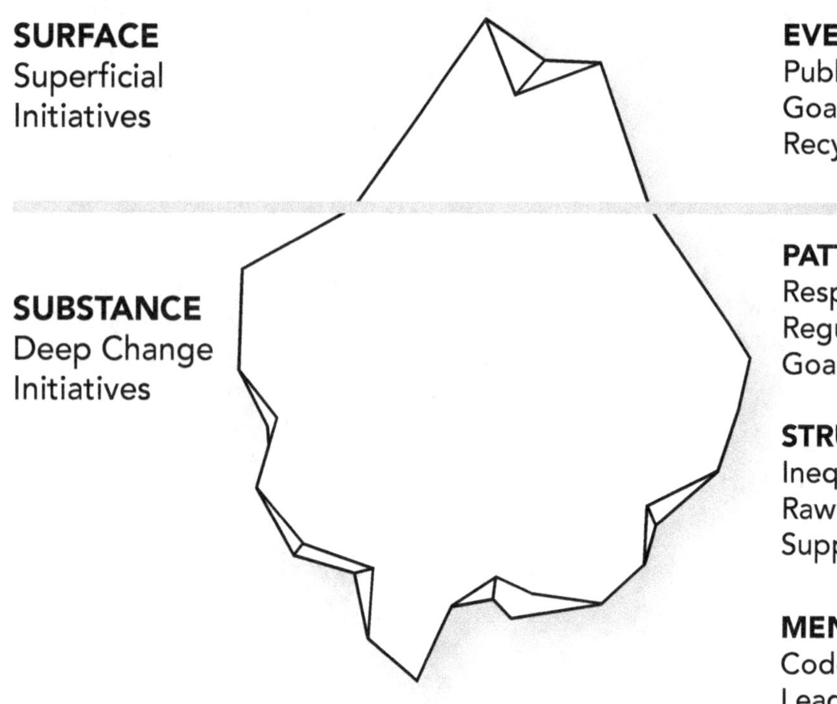

ICEBERG MODEL ADAPTED FROM EDWARD T. HALL, 1976

With the pandemic, climate change, the global waste crisis, supply chain disruptions and massive technological shifts all putting pressure on the ways that companies operate and society evolves, you'll distinguish yourself as proactive leaders and problem solvers, rather than problem avoiders and planet destroyers.

So, go ahead and abandon old and outdated ideas that sustainability is for hippies or just a "do-the-right-thing" approach, or that it's someone else's job, and instead see it for the innovation and leadership opportunity that it is.

All parameters and constraints placed upon us by nature's limits can be used as the guidelines and structures that fuel and foster true innovation. By flipping the mental switch to an opportunity mindset, you will illuminate the incredible potential that sustainability provides us all. With this open mindset, you can progress through these pages with an inspired outlook for significant systems change and then make that happen for your colleagues, business, sector, industry and society.

WHAT IS "FULL SYSTEMS" SUSTAINABILITY?

Historically, addressing environmental concerns has been approached in often simplistic ways, such as labeling products as biodegradable, pushing recycling as the main solution and touting a carbon neutral status. But as our understanding of the scale and size of the problems we face has evolved, so too has our ability to address them.

That's what full systems sustainability offers: a deeper dive into the systems that create the issues, coupled with real cultural and organizational change, driven by actions that go well beyond the obvious.

This guidebook shows you how to push past the superficial first layer of operational impact reduction (which is still an important starting point), move through to the main impact areas of the product life cycle and business model design, then go even further to create the full system experience for your customers and stakeholders. This is what it will take for us to transform to a circular and sustainable economy — a shift in perspective and the activation of new ways of doing business in the 21st century.

SOCIAL AS WELL AS ENVIRONMENTAL IMPACTS

One of the often forgotten aspects of sustainability is social impact. Sustainability often evokes ideas of environmental protection, and whilst this is one of the critical aspects, so too is economic health and social equity.

To ensure that the actions you take are contributing to a just and fair world, there are many aspects of social impacts that you can assess and enhance.

These include looking at the health and well-being of workers across all aspects of your supply chain, ensuring that you don't participate in unfair labor anywhere along your value chain and that working conditions are safe and equitable, providing access to healthcare and time off for workers, looking at the cultural impacts of your products on the people

and communities they are serving, prohibiting identity and race from impeding workers' or customers' ability to live their lives freely and finally, verifying that countries you are gaining resources from are doing so in ethical ways (this is a big issue with rare Earth minerals in technology, for example).

These social impact aspects should be considered across all areas of your business, from your office workers to the people extracting the raw materials through to the conditions of the factories and subcontractors dotted along your supply chain.

Yes, this is a lot to consider, which is why supply chain mapping is critical. We will dive more into that in Part 3.

MOVING PAST GDP

Currently, our global economic measuring system of Gross Domestic Product (GDP) does not account for materials or services taken from nature in any capacity, whether it's before they enter into the mainstream economy or when pollution impacts a natural systems' ability to sustain itself.

All raw materials extracted from nature are taken without an account of the impact that they have on the systems that created the resources, which means ecosystem services have a value of nothing in our current GDP-based system. Thus, there is

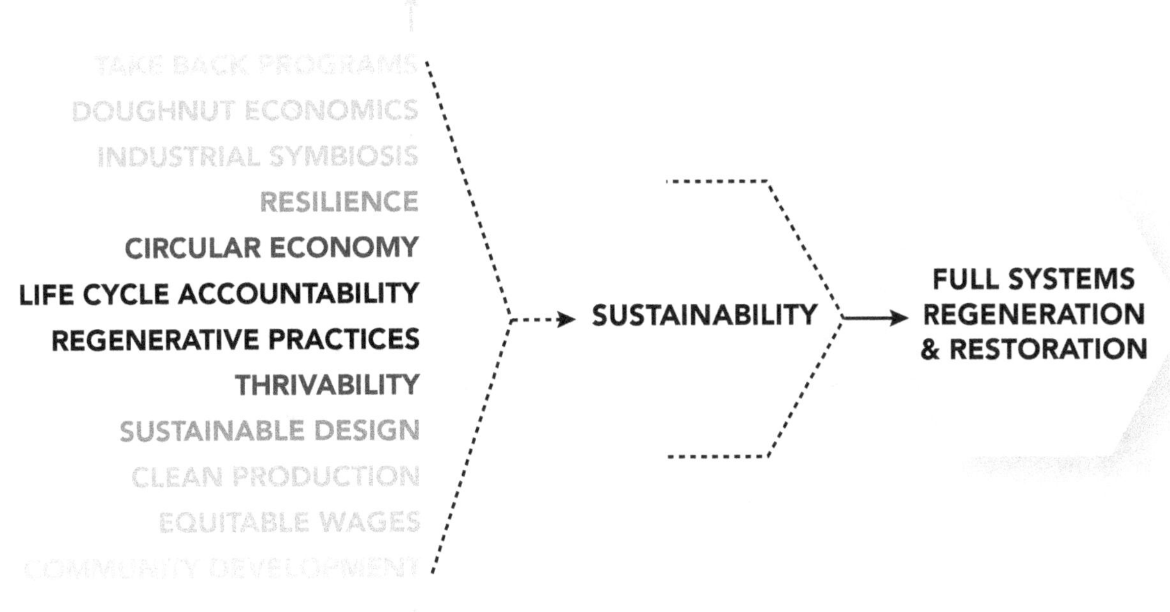

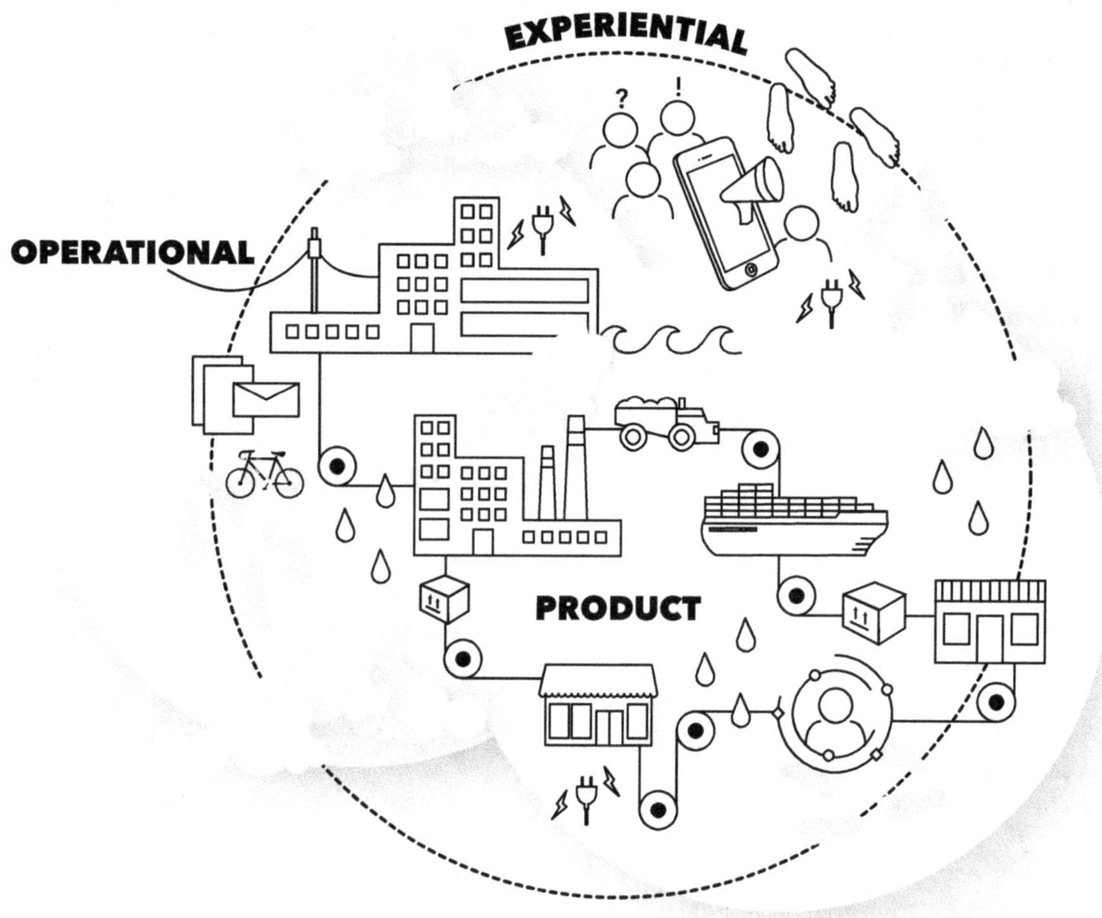

little economic incentive to reduce the exploitation of nature.

GDP only measures the activities of production and consumption inside the boundaries of a country. There is no assessment of losses, only gains. So, caretaking services provided by a family member have zero value in GDP, whereas paid childcare does. The loss of marine system health after an oil spill is not accounted for, but the cleanup effort after one registers as an increase in GDP.

There are many propositions (see next page) that seek to rectify this system failure, with some countries like New Zealand integrating wellness and other sustainability measurements into their GDP assessment.

ADDRESSING EXTERNALITIES

Economists have named the unaccounted-for aspects of an economy "externalities". These include things such as loss of eco-systems, pollution or the use of enslaved labor, for example.

> **"Half of the world's GDP is dependent on nature, and every dollar invested in restoration creates up to 30 dollars in economic benefits."**
>
> - United Nations Environment Program's "Becoming #GenerationRestoration" Report, 2021

Most externalities are negative, although some can be positive (such as an unaccounted-for benefit, but these are much more rare).

The issue with negative externalities is that the people who benefited from creating these are often not the ones who suffer the consequences of their negative effects.

This means there is little to zero incentive for the actors who inflict them on society to take action to alleviate the negative impacts they created (and economically benefited from) — hence the need for governments to create regulations that enforce responsibility for the negative actions (see the previous for a list of global actions to help rectify externalities).

The creators of externalities (such as companies) need to acknowledge the impacts of their actions and then redesign how they do business to account for and alleviate them. This is called extended producer responsibility or product stewardship. These are the fundamental ideas of doing impact assessment, which is a core part of a science-based approach to sustainability that this guidebook will walk you though.

DIFFERENT APPROACHES TO REDESIGNING GDP TO INCLUDE EQUITY AND WELLBEING

- **The Human Development Index** (HDI) is a statistical measurement tool developed by the United Nations to measure a country's overall achievement from a social and economic standpoint, based on the health of the people, their level of education and standard of living.

- **Genuine Progress Indicator** (GPI) was created in the US, and it takes into consideration the same things as GDP, but it adds on the cost of crime, ozone depletion and lost leisure time.

- **Thriving Places Index** (TPI) was developed by a charity in the UK; its primary focus is measuring the sustainability, equality and local conditions across 60 indicators.

- **Happy Planet Index** (HPI) from the New Economics Foundation looks at the ecological footprint, inequality, wellbeing and life expectancy of a country. Using available data from the UN and the Global Footprint Network, the index measures equality by looking at how evenly distributed wellbeing and life expectancy are across a country.

- **Better Life Index** (BLI) was developed by the Organization for Economic Cooperation and Development (OECD). They identified 12 measurable things essential to wellbeing: housing, income, jobs, community, education, environment, civic engagement, health, life satisfaction, safety and work-life balance.

- **The Social Progress Index** (SPI) assesses how well a country meets the social and environmental needs of their citizens.

- **Inclusive Development Index** (IDI) was proposed by the World Economic Forum (WEF) and adjusts GDP for measurements of unemployment. Productivity is included, as are figures for median income, inequality, poverty, healthy life expectancy, net savings rates and public debt. Carbon intensity is measured as well.

- **Living Standards Framework** (LSF) measures wellbeing, cultural identity, environment, income, consumption and social connections, providing an overall index of a nation's performance.

EXAMPLES OF GLOBAL REGULATIONS THAT ARE DRIVING SUSTAINABILITY TRANSFORMATION

- **UN Framework Convention on Climate Change** (UNFCCC): This is the basic legal framework and principles for international climate change cooperation to stabilize to avoid dangerous levels of atmospheric concentrations of GHGs. Under the treaty, industrialized countries are expected to be in the forefront of reducing emissions, they have agreed to provide financial support to developing countries to mitigate the impact of climate change, and have to report regularly on their climate change policies.

- **Restriction of Hazardous Substances** (RoHS): Developed by the European Union in 2002, this restricts the use of six known substances hazardous to human health and the environment for use in electrical equipment.

- **Basel Convention**: Signed in 1992, this is for the reduction of hazardous waste generation and the restriction of moving hazardous wastes internationally, except where it can be done in accordance with principles of sound environmental management. This applies to electronic waste since it contains hazardous materials.

- **The Montreal Protocol**: Signed in 1987 and often referred to as one of the most successful international environmental agreements, this set binding commitments to phase out use of 96 ozone depleting substances, such as chlorofluorocarbons (CFCs) and hydrofluorocarbons (HFCs).

- **Global Plastics Treaty**: UN Member States endorsed this landmark agreement in 2022 that addresses the full lifecycle of plastic from source to sea. It will come into force in 2024.
- **International Tropical Timber Agreement** (ITTA): This deals with the international trade in tropical timber to promote the use of sustainably-managed sources and reduce the market for legally-harvested forest products.

- **European Union Taxonomy for Sustainable Activities**: It came into force in July 2020 as part of the European Green Deal and establishes the basis for the EU taxonomy for ESG reporting by providing companies, investors and policymakers with appropriate definitions and conditions on what criteria an economic activity has to meet in order to qualify as being environmentally sustainable.

- **EU's Corporate Sustainability Due Diligence**: Adopted in 2022, this directive will foster sustainable and responsible corporate behavior by requiring companies' operations and corporate governance to include human rights and environmental considerations. The rules ensure businesses address adverse impacts of their actions across their value chains in and outside Europe. This does not apply to micro companies or Small and Medium-sized Enterprises (SMEs).

ACTIVE LEADERSHIP

It's easy to say you will do something and harder to actually do it. To address the issues of our time, we need a diversity of actions that lead to impact, transformation and systems-wide change. This requires leaders who are willing to think and behave in entirely new ways about delivering value, creating economic opportunities and designing business models.

Everything worth doing requires work, and any good leader knows that the more effort you put in, the greater the reward. There is so much unlocked potential for positive change; it just requires more people paving the way, showing what is possible and creating new types of normal.

Leaders are made through their actions, not just the things they say!

REMEMBER, IT'S A JOURNEY

Whether you are just getting started or already well along your sustainability journey, remember that this is a process of transformation. For every organization, small or large, it's not as though you can suddenly flip a switch and redesign your entire business overnight — this is a process of learning, experimenting, learning and evolving.

If it were easy, then it would have been done already. The opportunity is in doing the work to get to the insights that lead to better outcomes. This is the same in any innovation process: explore the potential to better understand it and then make changes that result in improved offerings.

Sustainability is a movement, a mindset and a process of transformation though stages of change.

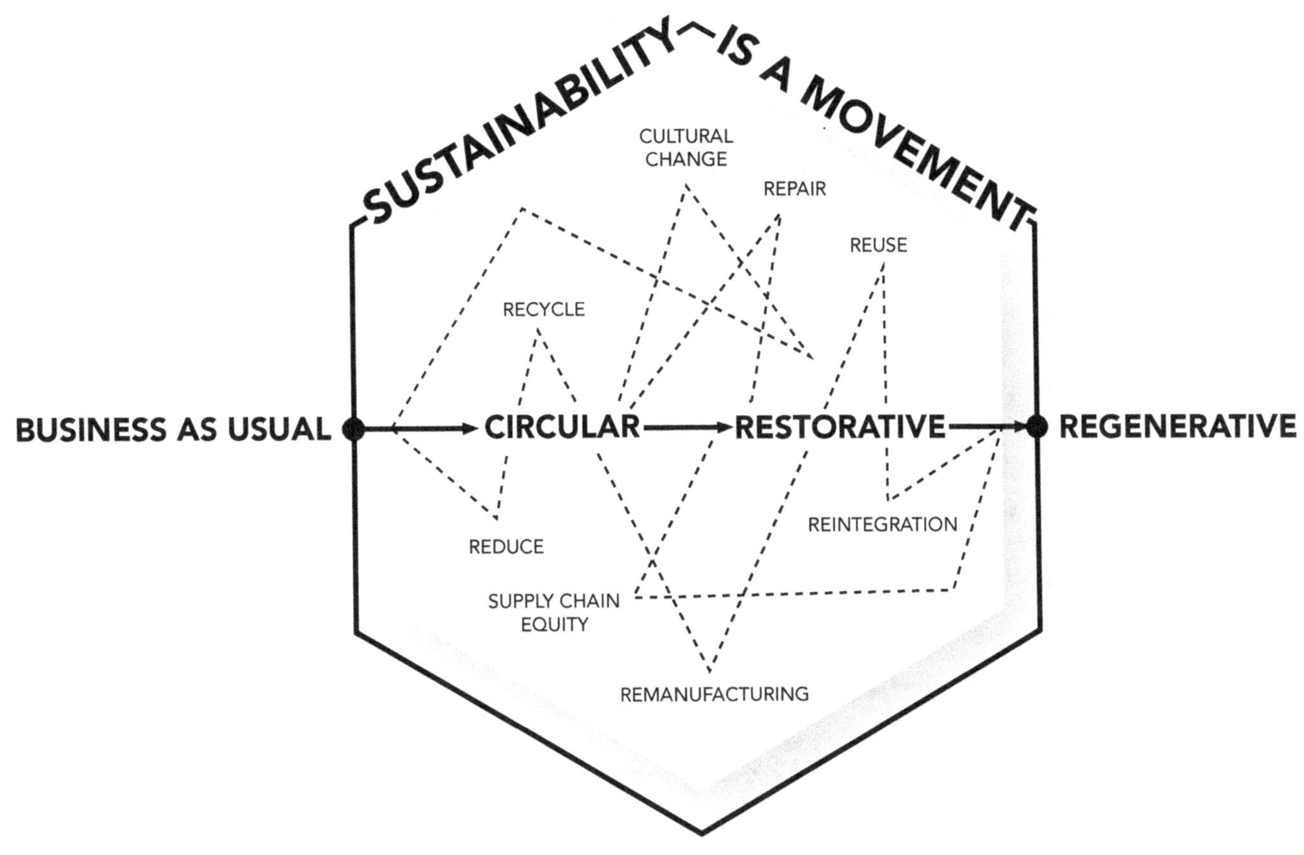

A WHOLE SHIFT IN PERSPECTIVE

The way we have done things for the last 75 years has been one of the main drivers of unsustainability on our shared planet. So first and foremost, sustainability is a framework for shifting perspective on where value lies and how we can create it in entirely new ways. Be it through a circular economy, regenerative agriculture or ending slavery in the supply chain, this requires abandoning the past's thinking paradigms that drove us into the current status quo so that new ways of operating, thinking and creating can emerge.

A SET OF TECHNICAL SKILLS

Whilst some people may think sustainability is just a movement toward doing better in business and life, it's also a set of technical skills that are required to assess, transform and advance unsustainable systems. From environmental auditing through to life cycle assessment, there are a suite of tools that enable businesses to integrate sustainability into their operations and long term planning. We will be covering many of these in the following sections of this guidebook.

WORKING WITHIN LIMITATIONS

The planet has ecological boundaries that, once crossed, can cause collapse, which leads to ecological and social disruption. Human communities are not dissimilar in having limits to growth. Knowing that there are safe operating spaces for humanity to flourish on the planet supports the approach of sustainability being based on firstly overcoming the current trend of ignoring limitations, and then advancing toward restoring the systems that have had their boundaries already breached, such as the climate.

TRANSFORMATION TOWARD A BETTER FUTURE

By learning from past actions that have had unintended consequences, we can develop new ways of meeting human needs, creating value and fueling the economy that are firstly sustainable, then restorative and regenerative. Sustainability is a process of transformation, so wherever you are at now, your current position should not be the end of your actions — it's the beginning. The journey to a better future is always ongoing. There are always better options just around the corner, especially as technology and new services arise. Be willing to pioneer change.

UNDERSTANDING AND TRANSFORMING IMPACTS

Everything we do has an impact on the planet, so the crux of a sustainability approach is to understand all the hidden impacts that occur as a result of business activities and then to redesign the systems, products, processes and supply chains to dramatically change negative impacts and create net positive outcomes.

A PATHWAY OF RESTORATION TOWARD REGENERATION

Sustainability offers practical tools, but regeneration is the goal. It's no longer enough to simply do no harm — we need to focus our end goals on actively restoring and regenerating the systems from which we've been taking so much from.

ABOUT SUSTAINING THE STATUS QUO

The word sustainability can be used to describe many things, from sustaining investments to sustainable investing — two things that have very different meanings! Like any word in the English language, it can be confused and misused, co-opted or just plain overused. Sustainability as a concept in relation to social, economic and environmental change is about the opposite of an unsustainable system, like the current linear, exploiting one that our economy is based on, the status quo system. Sustainability is not about sustaining the status quo; it's about disrupting it entirely and replacing it with a better operating system that meets the needs of all humans in equitable, just and sustainable ways.

ABOUT GREEN, ECO, TREE-HUGGING STUFF

The image that often comes to mind when people hear the word sustainability is green, recyclable, eco, panda bears, people hugging trees and the age-old hippie idea. This is changing, but the legacy images stick around (try searching for sustainability images now and you will still get a lot of outdated, green, earthy images!).

TOKENISTIC OR SUPERFICIAL

The days of doing superficial green actions are behind us; people are no longer easily fooled by simplistic and disingenuous approaches of making something green for marketing outcomes. Sustainability is about accepting your impacts on the world and ensuring that you are progressing toward rectifying them in significant and comprehensive ways.

JUST ABOUT RECYCLING

Another outdated trope is that sustainability is about making sure that products are recyclable and that offices have recycling. Recycling is part of the problem, as it has incentivized the creation of waste and perpetuated a very unsustainable system. Of course, recycling is part of the set of solutions that we need to address the waste crisis, but it should only be one of the last resorts. Before recycling, there are strategies like reuse, recapture, repair and remanufacture to try first.

HYPER-FOCUSED ON CARBON REDUCTION

Climate change is a major issue, but it is not the only thing that we need to respond to when it comes to sustainability. Carbon impacts are part of a full suite of impacts and issues that need to be addressed. Getting carbon tunnel vision, or only seeing the issues as being about reducing a carbon footprint or achieving net zero, is not full systems sustainability.

A SIMPLE THING YOU CAN JUST ADD ON TO WHAT YOU ARE ALREADY DOING

Sustainability is about understanding impacts and doing the work to rectify them. That means there will be discoveries of underlying issues that need to be addressed, new ideas and processes generated and policies followed. You can't just add sustainability on to what you are already doing, as this creates a bandaid. It needs to be integrated into your DNA so that staff, stakeholders and customers all see your sincerity and commitment.

WORKSHEETS

A common myth about sustainability is that it's just about "doing good" when in actual fact, it draws fundamentally on science and innovation as the foundations for transforming the way we do things. So yes, these transformations are better for the planet and people — but measurably better, and significantly so. To support this work, there are many worksheets included in this guidebook to be done individually or in teams.

<table>
<tr><td>PAST CHANGE IDENTIFICATION</td><td>Map out the current status quo of your industry. Explore what has changed and what the influencing factors are.</td></tr>
</table>

PAST CHANGES IN OUR ORGANIZATION & INDUSTRY

THE CURRENT STATUS QUO

____________________________ ____________________________

____________________________ ____________________________

____________________________ ____________________________

HOW WAS IT CHANGED?

____________________________ ____________________________

____________________________ ____________________________

____________________________ ____________________________

WHAT WERE THE CHANGE FACTORS & INFLUENCES?

____________________________ ____________________________

____________________________ ____________________________

____________________________ ____________________________

<table>
<tr><td>FUTURE CHANGE IDENTIFICATION</td><td>Map out the new sustainability focused approach. Explore how it could happen; what opportunities and influencing factors need to be in place?</td></tr>
</table>

FUTURE OPPORTUNITIES IN OUR ORGANIZATION & INDUSTRY

THE NEW APPROACH

______________________   ______________________

______________________   ______________________

______________________   ______________________

______________________   ______________________

HOW COULD IT BE BROUGHT ABOUT?

______________________   ______________________

______________________   ______________________

______________________   ______________________

______________________   ______________________

WHAT ARE THE CHANGE FACTORS, OPPORTUNITIES & INFLUENCES?

______________________   ______________________

______________________   ______________________

______________________   ______________________

______________________   ______________________

AN OVERVIEW OF YOUR SUSTAINABILITY JOURNEY

REFLECT

On a scale from 1-10, how confident are you talking about sustainability in business? Why did you gave yourself that rating?

GOAL

Establish the baseline of familiarity with both your personal and your team's understanding of sustainability in business. It also provides an opportunity for individual team members to consider where they are on their personal sustainability journey.

1-HOUR WORKSHOP IDEA

Dive into the past, present and future of your organization's sustainability journey. Use these question prompts to frame your exploration:

1. How have you approached sustainability up to this point?
2. What are your present motivations to improve?
3. Where do you want to see your company going in terms of sustainability goals?
4. If you have published values or mission statements, how do they reflect your sustainability goals?

You can use your answers to create your own Organizational Sustainability SWOT (Strengths, Weaknesses, Opportunities, Threats) chart to pull it all together.

☐ DATE COMPLETED ________________________________

1.2 THE FOUNDATIONS OF SUSTAINABILITY

THE LONG HISTORY OF SUSTAINABILITY

The term sustainability as it is used today comes in part from the Brundtland Commission's 1987 report "Our Common Future". This UN report laid out the goal of sustainable development as development that meets the needs of current generations without negatively affecting the ability for future generations to meet their own needs.

Prior to this, the idea of sustaining our species inline with the resources provided by nature can be traced back to the 17th century, where it was used in relation to responsible resource management (for example, forestry). For as long as humans have been taking from nature, the challenge of doing so in a way that maintains instead of exploits the resources has been a challenge.

Self-interest, market demands and economic drivers often push humans to take more than the system can give up without created irreversible damage. This is called the tragedy of the commons, where common resources are exploited for individual gains. Think of how this applies to the oceans, for example.

Nowadays, sustainability has become the shorthand term used to describe a range of actions, ideas and approaches based on the aspiration of intergenerational equity — which means making choices today that will result in a better future for current and upcoming generations. It's fundamentally about understanding the impacts of actions and designing solutions that move beyond the current economic status quo of exploitation and extraction, to bring the social and environmental impacts of our actions inline with the economic ones.

Scientists and researchers have long shown how human activity is causing significant impacts on the natural systems that sustain life (Lovelock, 2003). Thus, the risk of us collectively creating an unsustainable future is now a driving force for the

3 PILLARS OF SUSTAINABILITY

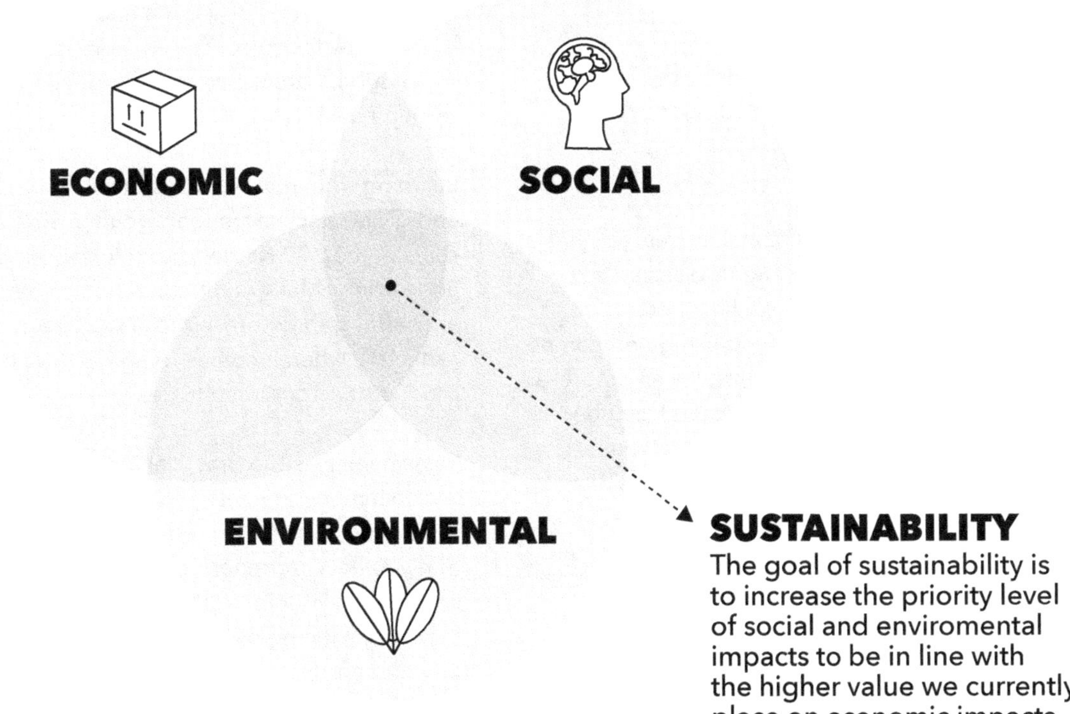

modern sustainability movement. This has meant governments are making laws, companies changing their ways and individuals looking for products and services that support a more sustainable lifestyle.

We are now at a point in human history where our actions are threatening to derail our civilization. Climate change disrupting the weather in catastrophic ways, ocean plastic bioaccumulating up the food chain and into our blood streams, air pollution is killing 9 million people every year (Fuller et al, 2022) — even the pandemic is linked to habitat destruction (Gillespie, et al, 2021). Not to mention climate change, water scarcity and soil degradation are threatening our ability to produce enough food (Molotoks et al, 2021).

Even though awareness and desire for action is increasing, the calls to reduce Greenhouse Gas (GHG) emissions, change our addiction to disposable plastics and stop pumping chemicals into the atmosphere are not being heard by some sectors of society. Our common future depends on the actions we take today to drawdown carbon, shift disposables to reusables and change the way businesses create value in the economy.

To be able to sustain ourselves, we must change how we create goods and services, run companies, organize society and value nature. The shift starts with you and your business.

Nowadays, sustainability is a global movement that touches all aspects of society and involves an array of scientific and technical approaches that can be applied to understand impacts and design outcomes that rectify the problems of the past. It's an umbrella term used to describe different structural changes and actions inside businesses and government (carbon accounting, corporate social responsibility, sustainable supply chains, circular economy, etc.), in the financial sector (impact investing, ESG, etc.) and individual lifestyle choices (sustainable living, zero waste, etc.)

Due to its popularity, sustainability is often misused (resulting in greenwashing) and thus commonly

misunderstood (confusing people, which leads to distrust). This makes sustainability appear weak, complex and even overwhelming at times. But the original and withstanding idea is to rectify the unsustainable consequences of our actions so that we create the things we need without negative side effects to people and the natural world that we all rely on for life.

THE PUSH FOR REGENERATION

Sustainability as a movement is the process of shifting social values and reorienting away from exploitation toward a regenerative society, one where we give back more than we take. To get to this better state, we have to redesign all of our current processes, systems, businesses, services, products, lifestyles and mindsets.

Over the years of this movement's evolution, there have been many emergent aspects that connect and propel this thinking forward. The circular economy (Stahel, 2016) emerged as a leading approach to designing waste out of the system, and now we have the emergence of regenerative thinking and design.

Regeneration is what nature does. It is the building block for sustaining life on Earth. All parts of nature go through cycles of growth and renewal that enable new life to constantly form, and from organic adaptation, nature creates strength and resilience through each cycle.

Learning from nature, working within natural systems and giving back more than we take are fundamental shifts in the way we need to think about business and society. Many companies around the world are starting to embrace these significant shifts, especially when it comes to agriculture, buildings, products and community design.

Sustainability is the practical approach to understanding impacts and taking significant action to reduce, replace and redesign negative impacts that you have; regeneration in business is about fundamentally shifting the purpose that drives your business, aligning all of your actions to be impact-free and replenishing the systems that you take from.

THE ROLE OF NATURE IN SUSTAINABILITY

It's important to reflect and consider underlying issues with how we humans perceive nature and assign value to the services that nature provides. As mentioned, our GDP-based economic system ignores the value that nature provides, creating a low-value perception of nature for society. Because it's easy to waste things that we don't value, this perception legitimates the exploitation of nature.

Nature is not just something beautiful for us to enjoy; all humans intrinsically need nature. It makes up the entire living organism that is the planet and provides all the services that support life on Earth.

Without nature, no human or any other species of animal or plant would exist — we are all interconnected and interdependent with nature. This is not some hippie idea; it's a biophysical reality. Each of us are all part of the natural world.

In fact, humans make up just 0.01% of the world's biomass, with 83% of the world's biomass being made up of plants (Bar-On et al, 2018).

Despite this, human actions dominate all other aspects of the planet, to the point where scientists are now arguing that we have changed every aspect of the world and in the process, dramatically disrupted the way natural systems work together to sustain life (Crutzen, 2006).

Nature is a very efficient system whereby everything is cycled through other systems, helping to produce more life. There is no waste in nature. Humans are the ones who create products that are dangerous or damaging to us and natural systems. Thus, we can learn from the way nature solves problems.

This is a fundamental aspect of biomimicry and nature-based solutions approaches, as well as the underlying approach to regenerative thinking.

CONCEPT DEFINITIONS

BIOMIMICRY: An approach to creating products and services that mimics the way nature works by studying and replicating the solutions found in the natural world (Benyus, 1997). Examples include: aerodynamic blades on wind turbines mimicking the fin of a whale or bullet trains mimicking the beak of a bird.

BIOMIMETICS: An engineering and scientific approach that emulates the processes, models, elements and systems of nature to solve complex human problems.

BIOMORPHISM: Designs that are visually similar to patterns found in the natural world. These look like nature but don't have to perform the same way, whereas biomimicry and biomimetics copy the functions of natural systems.

BIOPHILIA: The concept that humans seek out connections with nature and other forms of life. This has turned into an approach for urban planning and building design that actively brings nature into the work environment for health and well-being benefits, natural climate control, better air quality and building designs that change behavior. Examples include: buildings with no air-conditioning designed around natural cooling processes, internal greenhouses and interior design that mimics nature's patterns.

NATURE-BASED SOLUTIONS: An approach that uses natural systems to actively restore nature or design solutions to meet human needs that are based on nature's resilience. Examples include: replanting oyster colonies to break up waves to protect coastal areas, reducing flooding via sponge cities and reintroducing beavers to dam rivers.

REGENERATIVE DESIGN: An approach to design that uses whole-systems thinking and creates processes that restore, revitalize and renew their own sources of energy and materials. Examples include: agricultural practices that restore soil, combine plants and rotate crops or buildings that generate their own energy, capture water, use it on site and filter it for reuse.

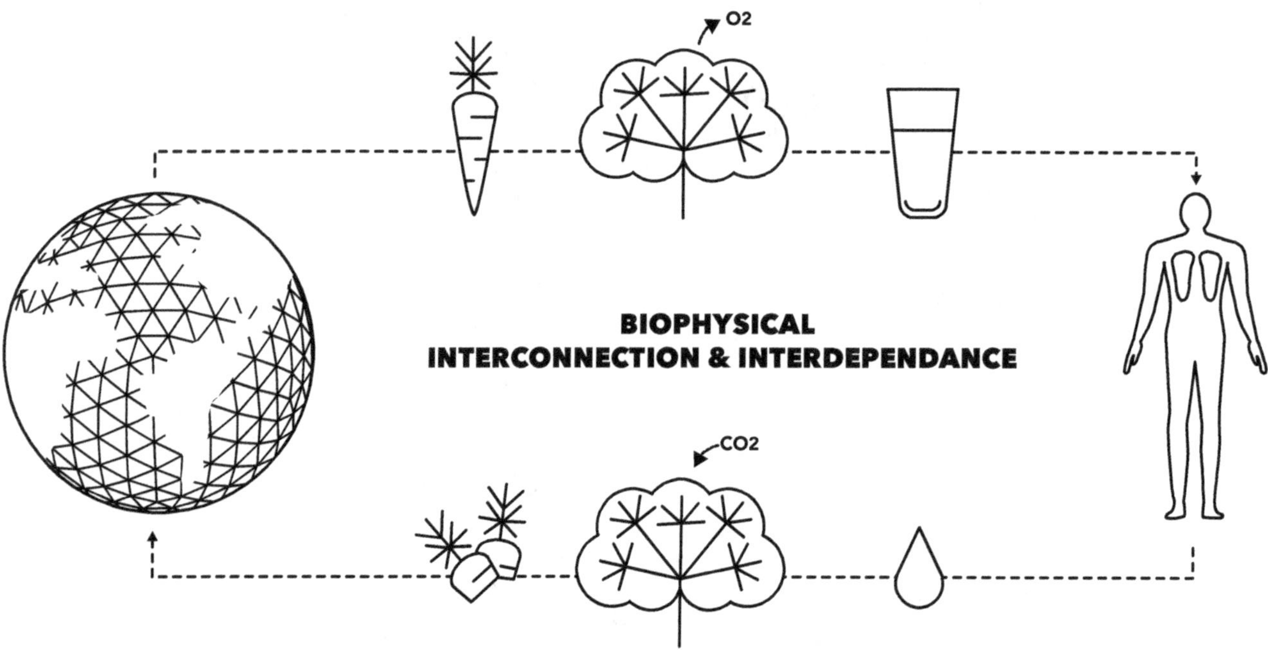

REFLECTION ACTIVITY

REFRAMING SUSTAINABILITY AT WORK

REFLECT

What misconceptions about sustainability do you hold? Write a list of all the things that come to mind when you think about sustainability, and consider where these ideas came from? What could you do right now to help expand your viewpoint and rewrite old ideas with new approaches? Use the prompt below or make your own.

GOAL

This reflection helps you dismantle previously-held ideas about sustainability that can prevent you from activating full systems sustainability to your full potential. Articulating how you can reframe it helps bring your new understanding full circle so that you can move forward more confidently. And finally, benchmarking the actions that other organizations in your industry have taken can help give you ideas on getting started.

REFRAME

I used to think that sustainability was ______________________ because ____________________; now I understand that it's ____.

1-HOUR WORKSHOP IDEA

Using the worksheet on the next page, benchmark organizations within your industry that have been leading the way and identify actions that could work for your organization.

☐ DATE COMPLETED ________________________________

TRANSFORMATIONS IN THE ECONOMY

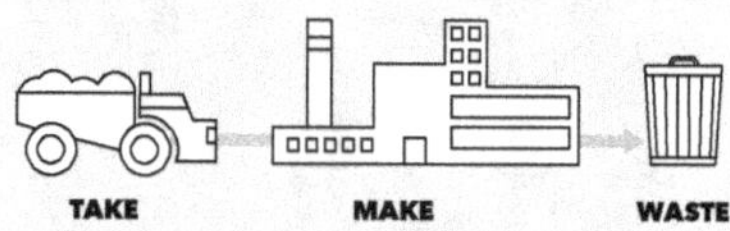

THE LINEAR ECONOMY

This is the current "take, make, waste" model of economic growth that has dominated the way we run the economy and do business to date. It's called linear because it churns through resources, producing waste whilst not considering the losses associated with this one-directional model.

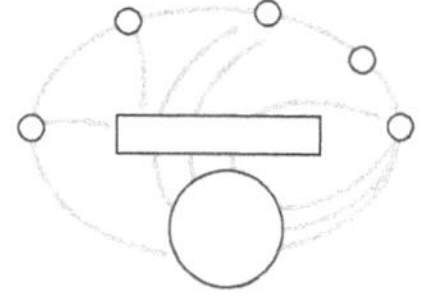

THE CIRCULAR ECONOMY

An alternative approach to business, product design and the organization of society that intentionally eliminates waste and pollution by closing the loop from linear to circular. This involves keeping products and materials in perpetual use or using appropriate remanufacturing, repair and recycling whilst designing all aspects of society to support and regenerate natural systems.

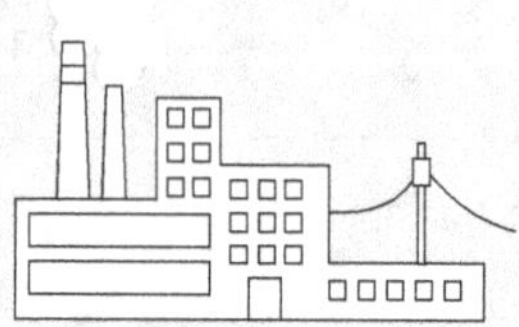

BUSINESS AS USUAL

The current extractive, linear model limits consideration of the impact that actions have outside of the economic benefits. The status quo is growth regardless of the negative externalities whereby short-term gains are prioritized over long term impacts. This is a very short-sighted, exploitative way of running a business.

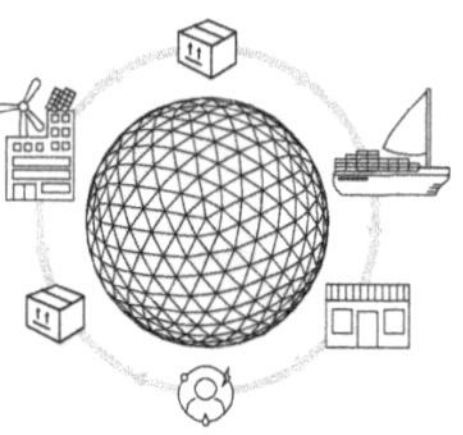

SUSTAINABLE

The ability for a system to sustain itself without negative effects. In order for something to be sustainable, it must have all of the ingredients for restoration and renewal. The current linear economy is unsustainable by design, as it takes and wastes more from the system, then doesn't leave enough for restoration. In the business context, being sustainable requires transforming the DNA of a business so that it does not create negative externalities.

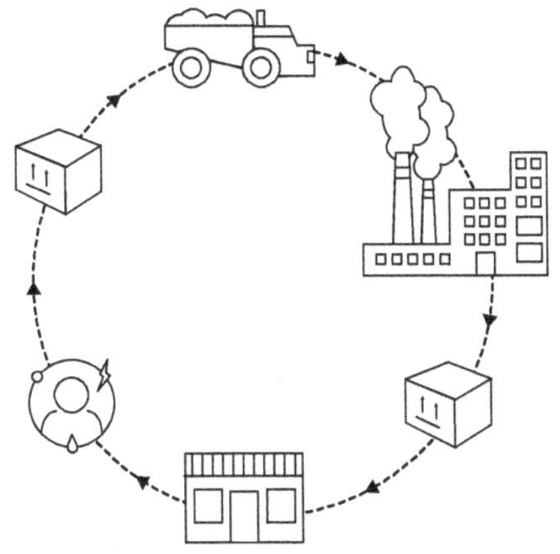

CIRCULAR

Redesigning business models to take back waste by designing pollution and negative impacts out of the system right from the start. A circular economy is resource efficient and designed to cycle value around a closed loop system.

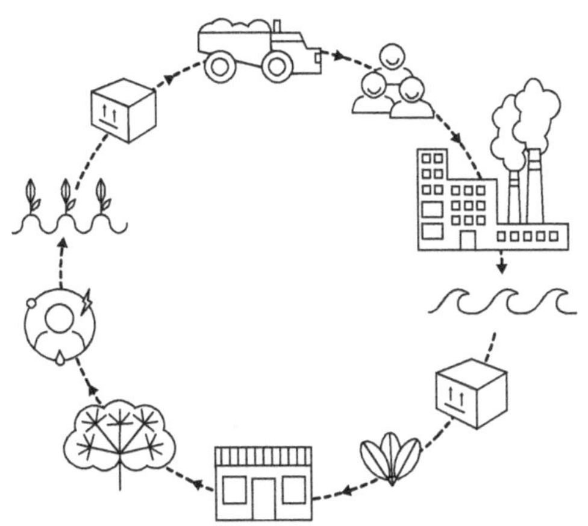

RESTORATIVE

Actively contributing to restoring and repairing ecological systems that have been destroyed or damaged through economic activity. This extends to natural and human communities being focused on restoring a state of health and wellbeing.

REGENERATIVE

An organization or being that gives back more than it takes through everything it does; this goes beyond circular and sustainable and provides additional value back to nature and society. It's a system that is designed to create ecological value over time.

<table>
<tr><td>BENCHMARKING LEADERS</td><td>Identify organizations in your industry that have been leading the way. Analyze the actions that set them apart and that your organization could take.</td></tr>
</table>

ORGANIZATIONS THAT HAVE LED THE WAY IN SUSTAINABILITY IN OUR INDUSTRY

ORGANIZATION A   **ORGANIZATION B**   **ORGANIZATION C**

TOP 5 ACTIONS THAT DEFINE THEIR LEADERSHIP IN OUR INDUSTRY

1.3 CORE SUSTAINABILITY CONCEPTS & THINKING SHIFTS

In this section, we'll journey through the high-level thinking tools relevant to advancing sustainability in business and society, exploring the current scientific understandings on why it's so important and urgent that we change the way human activities impact the planet.

THE ANTHROPOCENE AND PLANETARY BOUNDARIES

For over 11,500 years, humans have lived in a stable climatic period called the Holocene. This has allowed our species to grow our population, create settled societies, develop incredible technologies and control the planet to our advantage.

This has, however, come with many destructions and impacts to the planet's operating system, as the Earth is a giant living system that needs to be in balance for life to flourish. As a result of humans' collective activity, geologists have now defined a new geological epoch called The Anthropocene (Crutzen, 2006). With "anthro" meaning humans, as in Anthropology, this underscores how we humans have impacted every inch of the planet and is evidenced through Earth's geological records.

The argument is that since the Industrial Revolution and specifically since the economic growth of 1950s onwards, soot, aluminum, chemicals and nuclear isotopes have been laid down in the geological records of Earth, as evidenced through the rock, ice and sediment layers.

A set of graphs called the Great Acceleration Graphs (Steffen, 2015) show the hockey stick increase in humanity's growth at the same time as nature's decline. Earth Systems Scientists from the Stockholm Resilience Network have created a set of nine planetary boundaries (Stahel, 2016) that demonstrate the health of the planet and propose that once several of these boundaries are crossed, we could enter into ecological collapse.

GLOBAL TRENDS FROM THE GREAT ACCELERATION GRAPHS

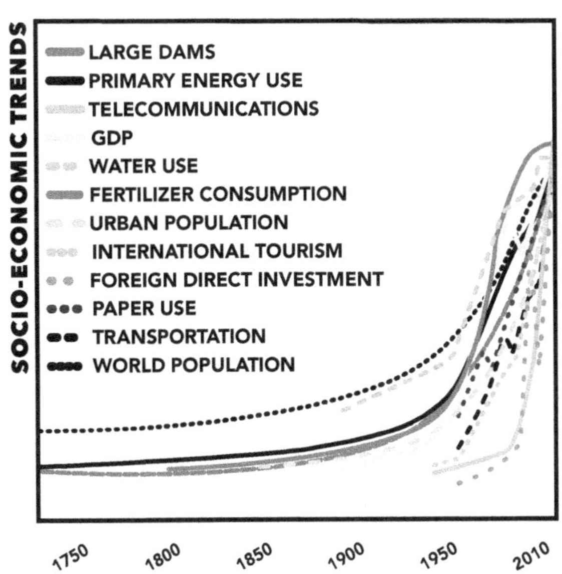

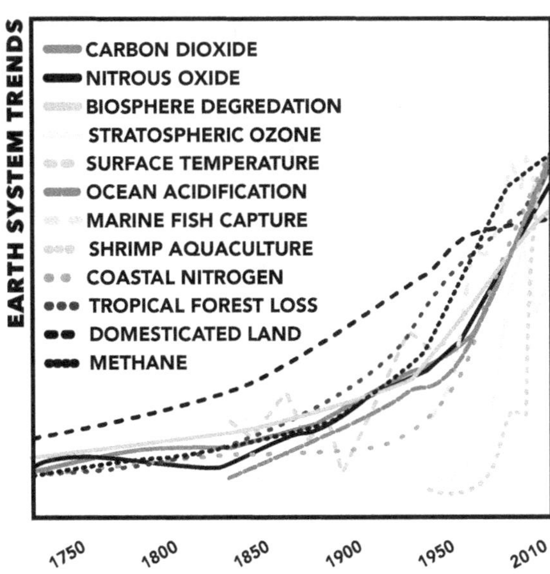

SOURCE: IGBD, 2015 International Geosphere-Biosphere Programme, Stockholm Resilience Centre, Steffen, W., W. Broadgate, L. Deutsch, O. Gaffney and C. Ludwig (2014), The Trajectory of the Anthropocene: the Great Acceleration, Submitted to The Anthropocene Review

ECOLOGICAL FOOTPRINTS

There are several different ways of measuring the impact of our actions on the planet. One well-respected method is the Ecological Footprint Methodology (Wackernagel, 1998). This looks at the amount of biologically productive area that is needed to provide the required resources (such as land for agriculture and materials for houses) to sustain the population of a community, country and the entire planet.

This is a method of gauging humanity's dependence on natural resources; it provides a simple calculation about how much of the environment is needed to sustain a particular lifestyle. Since it often compares the lifestyles of people from different countries, it shows that people in higher consumption societies have a much larger ecological footprint than those with lower consumption and globalization.
It was developed in the 1990s and is a well-respected way of assessing and understanding the ecological demands of individual actions.
You can go online right now and do your own personal ecological footprint assessment (www.footprintcalculator.org); you'll probably find that supporting your lifestyle requires the resources of 3-6 Earths!

The global average right now is 1.7 planets. And every year, there is a date called Earth Overshoot Day, which indicates the day on the calendar when we have collectively used up more resources than the Earth can replenish. It is often held in July for the entire planet, but each country has a different date. For example, Canada and Finland are in March, New Zealand is in April, Portugal and France in May, Thailand in September and Ecuador in December. The later your date, the more sustainable your country is.

It was around the late 1970s when we started to extract, use and waste more resources than the Earth could replenish. As you can see from the graph above, this has worsened year-on-year, except when we have global economic slow-downs that cause the rate of extraction to decrease. But then there are often rebounds that follow.

ECOLOGICAL FOOTPRINT IMPACT CATEGORIES

BUILT LAND	**HOUSING** **ROADS** **ENERGY SUPPLY**
AGRICULTURE	**HUMAN & ANIMAL FOOD CROPS** **BIOFUELS** **PLANT BASED TEXTILES**
FORESTRY	**LOGGING & CONSTRUCTION** **CONSUMER PRODUCTS** **PACKAGING**
WATER BASED RESOURCES	**OCEANS & RIVERS** **FISH FARMS** **HYDRO POWER**
LAND BASED RESOURCES	**MEAT & DAIRY ANIMALS** **GRAZING LAND** **ANIMAL BASED TEXTILES**
FOSSIL FUELS	**MANUFACTURING & TRANSPORTATION** **HEATING & COOLING** **OIL BASED TEXTILES**

SOURCE: footprintnetwork.org

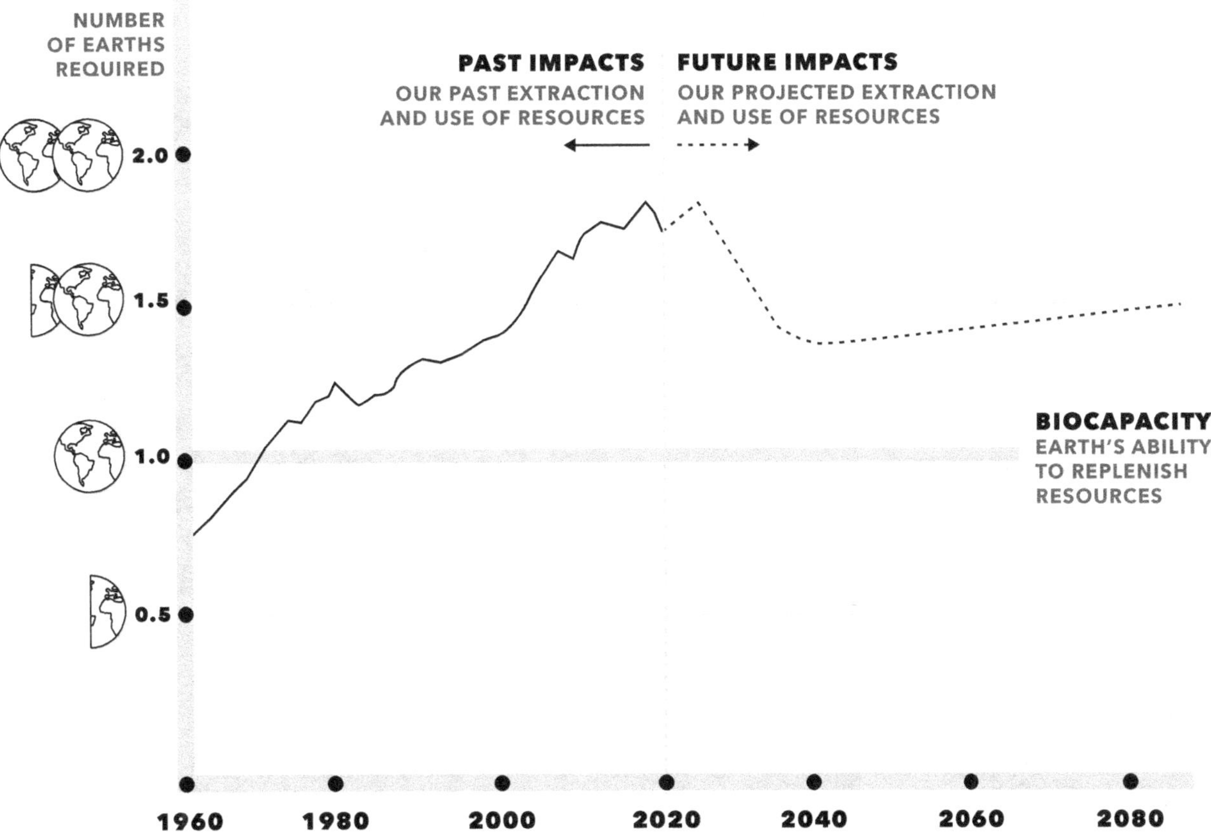

SOURCE: footprintnetwork.org

This means we live in an ecological deficit, so we have to find innovative ways to meet our human needs while maintaining and respecting the life support systems that we currently have on Earth. This is one of the fundamental ideas of sustainability: get the jagged impact line down to meet the biocapacity of Earth line.

The measurement of resource requirements is done through global hectares (GHA), and a country or city is considered unsustainable if its demand for natural resources is greater than what it can supply itself. Most modern economies are unsustainable.

Biocapacity is the ability of areas to continuously renew resources or be regenerated. The capacity for ecosystems to regenerate is being threatened by extraction but also by the effects of climate change (Cavicchioli et al, 2019).

The Ecological Footprint Methodology allows us to see how individual actions accumulate to have big impacts on the natural systems that sustain us. It is a very useful tool to gain perspective on how your choices add to community, country and planetary impacts. Once you do yours, see what changes you need to make to your lifestyle to live within the means of one planet!

BIODIVERSITY

Biodiversity defines the variety and complexity of life on Earth. It includes all the plants, bacteria, animals and fungi that live in the biosphere, which is the zone of life between the depths of the ocean and the tips of the atmosphere.

Biodiversity can be measured and is often defined by a classification of communities of similar life forms or locations and interrelationships. There are an estimated 8.7 million species on Earth, with only 1.2 million having been identified by humans so far (Mora et al, 2011).

Biodiversity is what makes ecosystems complex and resilient. Every ecosystem is made up of individual entities that work together to sustain the system as a whole. These then provide free services, such as cleaning the air, purifying water, producing food, cycling nutrients and storing carbon — all things that enable life to flourish. These are called ecosystem services.

ECOSYSTEM SERVICES

These are the intangible services provided for "free" by nature, like fresh water to drink, food to eat and materials to build and make fuel, medicines, etc. These services also include climate regulation and natural defenses like flood or landslide protection provided by tree covering in forests or mangroves protecting coastlines.

From an economic standpoint, the elements that make up a natural system can be defined as a form of capital. This is the idea of Natural Capital, originally put forth in the 1973 book "Small is Beautiful" by E.F. Schumacher and further developed by environmental economics.

NATURAL CAPITAL

Natural capital is a concept of natural systems having economic value, with all the world's natural asset stocks like soil, water, air, geology and all living things being accounted for in a way that helps to sustain and respect them (Costanza, 1997). From

EXAMPLES OF ECOSYSTEM SERVICES

BUILT ENVIRONMENT

BUILDING MATERIALS SUCH
AS WOOD, STEEL, & CLAY
CLIMATE CONTROL THROUGH
SHADE

AGRICULTURE

NITROGEN
PHOSPHORUS
FRESH WATER
CARBON SEQUESTRATION
PHOTOSYNTHESIS

ANIMALS

MEAT & DAIRY
MATERIALS SUCH AS
LEATHER, WOOL
& FUR
MEDICINE

FORESTS

WOOD PRODUCTS FOR
FURNITURE, PAPER
& FIREWOOD
CARBON STORAGE
HABITATS

WATER

FRESH DRINKING
WATER
HYGIENE
AGRICULTURE

OCEANS

FISH & SEAFOOD
CARBON SEQUESTERING
ALGAE
PHOTOSYNTHESIS

REFLECTION ACTIVITY

REGENERATION AT WORK

REFLECT

Consider 5 natural resources that your business depends on for your product and/or service offerings. What services do they currently offer as an untouched natural system, and what impact do you have on these?

Choose one to analyze for an initiative for regeneration (for example, if your business uses trees, consider where they come from, what services the forest currently provides and how you could ensure more trees than you use are protected or reforested).

GOAL

Connect how your business both relies on natural resources and uses them for profit. Begin to consider what regenerative actions you can take.

1-HOUR WORKSHOP IDEA

Explore the impacts of the main resources your company depends on by using the worksheet on the next page.

Create working groups or teams that are allocated a certain material. Have them research and report back on the key impacts and opportunities for evolving them or replacing the materials with more sustainable alternatives.

This will help you develop a knowledge bank on material level impacts.

☐ DATE COMPLETED ________________________________

<table>
<tr><td>DIVESTMENT OPPORTUNITIES</td><td>Consider all aspects of your social and environmental raw material impacts. How can you divest from using these?</td></tr>
</table>

**WHAT ARE THE LOWEST IMPACT
RAW MATERIALS THAT YOU CAN USE?**

**HOW CAN YOU DECARBONIZE
THIS PROCESS?**

**WHAT IS THE LOWEST IMPACT
WAY TO EXTRACT THEM?**

**WHAT OPPORTUNITIES FOR
REGENERATIVE PRACTICES ARE THERE?**

> **"Natural capital can be defined as the world's stocks of natural assets which include geology, soil, air, water and all living things"**
> - Natural Capital Forum

these ecosystems, humans derive all the resources they need to survive, thus creating an incentive to value them.

Resource extraction has tripled since 1970 (Oberle et al, 2019), and we use over 100 billion tons of raw materials extracted from nature every year (de Wit, 2020). There is a growing movement to account for natural capital in economic measures and to prevent unregulated markets from being incentivized to destroy natural systems (Hein et al, 2020).

One proposed approach is to put an economic value on natural stocks and the systems that they exist within. This value can then be used to account for the actions that humans take.

NATURE'S INTRINSIC VALUE

Nature has intrinsic value, which means that it has the inherent right to exist outside of a human value system.

The idea that something has inherent value regardless of economic definitions is a newer part of our collective thought. Since modernity, nature and all its resources have been seen as serving human needs as the priority, rather than nature having inherent value outside of that which we have defined.

This is a big part of what sustainability is seeking to normalize: nature and all living things having intrinsic worth and thus, rights. Anything we extract from nature is not just as valuable as the raw material, but it's also as valuable as the service that it provides as being part of the natural system.

For example, consider the ability of trees to sequester carbon. In order to harvest the wood to produce toilet paper, the forest is removed. In

OUR BIOSPHERE

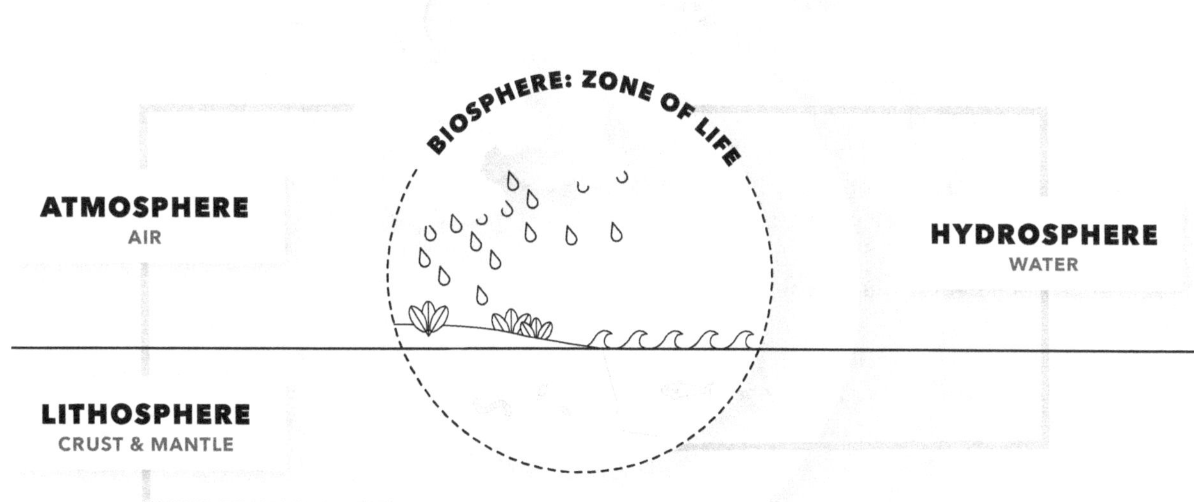

doing so, the forest's ability to sequester carbon, clean water, provide habitat or produce oxygen is eliminated. Currently these losses are not accounted for at all. But imagine if these ecosystem losses were subtracted from the economic gains that the producer would get from the toilet paper. Then, the true cost of the final product would be calculated. This would incentivize the production of less damaging products whilst retaining highly valuable ecosystems.

Valuing nature in a way that humans understand is a complex area that is still under debate. But somehow, we need to calculate the actions humans have against all of nature's intrinsic right to exist. We need to find a way to value nature.

VALUING NATURE'S SERVICES

Our desire to pay for something is often connected to our perceived gain from obtaining the thing we are seeking. This helps determine how we value it and thus how much we are willing to pay to have it.

Firstly, there are two use-based values:

DIRECT BENEFITS: The immediate benefits we get from taking stuff from nature, such as materials extracted from the ecosystem. Recreational uses, such as hiking, would also be seen as direct benefits.

INDIRECT BENEFITS: The willingness to pay for a service because of the utility we get out of the system staying intact. This includes things like bees being valued because we get indirect benefits from their pollination. Indirect uses are often not as appreciated as direct benefits because they are harder to see and not as well understood.

Next, there are non-use values, which are less tangible:

BEQUEST VALUES: The long-term benefits that nature offers future generations if we keep the systems intact. This is about the cultural and long-term gains that come from not using up resources today.

THREE WAYS TO LEARN FROM NATURE

BE CONSTANTLY CURIOUS

Explore the way nature solves problems in your everyday life and remember that you are constantly interacting with all manners of nature's things, from plants to weather systems.

Learn to observe and identify the way nature solves problems and see how this can be incorporated into your decision making.

DEVELOP A SYSTEMS PERSPECTIVE

This is critical to understanding and working within the world in more productive ways.

By seeing the natural, social and industrial systems, you will get a more refined perspective on how the world works and how our actions affect the systems around us.

SEE THE WORLD AS FLOWS

The systems around us are constantly feeding into other systems, and everything is flowing through other things.

The world is made up of systems within systems; by seeing how these connect, you start to understand how things affect each other and how everything is interdependent and interconnected!

OBSERVING CIRCULAR SYSTEMS IN NATURE

REFLECT

Take 10 minutes to go outside and find an example of a circular and regenerative system in action in nature. Consider how nature uses all of its waste in the process. What insights you can learn from the observations?

GOAL

Begin learning from nature's design solutions so you can bring nature-based solutions into your organization.

1-HOUR WORKSHOP IDEA

Use the worksheet below as a guide to work as a team in observing and discussing some of nature's circular and regenerative systems.

INPUTS   **OUTPUTS**

☐ DATE COMPLETED ____________________________________

EXISTENCE VALUES: This refers to the satisfaction that you get from knowing something continues to exist — for example, knowing that whales exist, even if you will never see one in person.

OPTION VALUES: These exist in some markets where there is an option to potentially use something in the future. The idea that you may one day need access to nature increases your willingness to pay for its preservation today.

Sustainability requires us to have a clear account of natural capital depreciation that occurs as a result of business activities and thus, there is a need to value natural capital changes (Azqueta & Sotelsek, 2007).

But this is often complicated, as different categories of defining the value of nature will result in different calculations. There is also the idea that nature has its own value, separate to human measurement tools. The concept that nature has the right to exist has been tested in courts in New Zealand with the movement for nature to be given personhood. The Whanganui River in New Zealand has been granted this status.

LEARNING FROM NATURE

An important thinking shift when developing a full systems perspective on sustainability is accepting that humans are biological beings who are deeply interconnected with and part of nature.

We are all dependent on natural systems, as we have to inhale oxygen every few seconds, fuel our bodies with food several times a day and drink fresh water to survive. No one can avoid the biological necessities of being human, and this means we all have a deep connection with the planet and the resources it provides us.

Despite this, we have managed to design many of our systems to be so industrially removed that we have forgotten how to learn from nature, eliminating the ability to discover how the planet solves problems so efficiently and beautifully. Learning to see and respect nature's intelligence allows an approach to restorative and regenerative thinking that looks to nature for insights on how to solve human-created problems in sustainable and regenerative ways.

Nature cycles resources and never creates waste, whereas in our human-created system, we waste resources and have built a system based on waste. Since everything comes from nature, it must at some point return, often in the form of pollutants that can't be reabsorbed back into nature in benign ways, like all plastics. If you look to nature for inspiration and insights, you will see nature has a role for everything.

The saying, "There is no away," reminds us that we can never really throw things away because there is no away on this closed biosphere we all share.

The planet is not an infinite sink where we can pump out pollution and waste without it eventually coming back to impact us all. Just look at the ocean plastic waste disaster — this has all happened in the last 30 years.

As such, your business decisions need to be considerate of the natural systems you are drawing upon and explore ways to return a positive contribution at the end of life of your productions.

Learning from nature and understanding natural systems is one of the approaches being used by forward-thinking companies and is called nature-based solutions.

CLIMATE CHANGE

Climate change, also referred to as global warming, is the main term used to describe the Greenhouse Effect, which is the increase in heat-trapping gases such as methane and carbon dioxide that are released into the atmosphere by human activity.

These gases accumulate, creating a glasshouse effect over the Earth whereby heat from the sun can't escape back into space, resulting in the surface of the Earth warming. Current expectations are that we will reach 2.3°C warmer. It doesn't sound like much, but it's the cumulative effects that cause the most concerns.

Climate change is an obvious symptom of the Anthropocene, as it can be directly linked to human activity since the birth of the Industrial Revolution. Since then, humans have extracted and burned significant amounts of fossil fuels like oil, gas and coal, which are made up of stored carbon over millions of years. When burned, this releases the locked-in carbon dioxide back into the atmosphere as gases at a faster rate than the Earth's systems can reabsorb them.

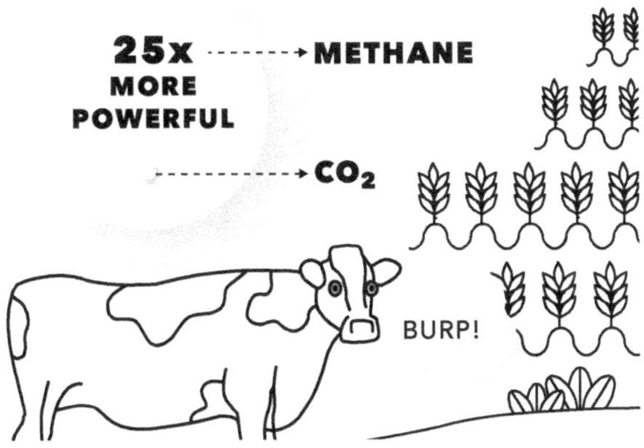

Carbon is a natural part of the Earth's systems. It's absorbed and cycled round by trees, plants and ocean phytoplankton. They convert it into oxygen that humans and other breathing animals inhale; we then exhale carbon dioxide. But the issue we are collectively facing now has to do with the excessive amount released in a relatively short period of time, coupled with the rate of nature's destruction. Thus, we don't have the natural systems drawing down carbon and locking it up at the same rate we have released it.

This build-up of excess greenhouse gasses has resulted in dramatic changes to the cycles and systems that make the planet work. The oceans are getting warmer, which leads to more frequent and extreme weather events.

Especially in the last few years, we've broken many heat records with temperatures getting more extreme (hot and cold). This leads to wildfires, heat waves and droughts, which reduces our collective security since we can't produce enough food,

access water or live in many areas of the world due to the threats of rising sea levels and extreme heat. Aside from the emissions from tailpipes and smokestacks, climate change impacts are embedded in everything we create and do. Every email we send, each piece of technology we own and all the food we eat has embodied carbon impacts. So when seeking to address the impacts that actions have on the climate, we have to expand our understanding of what it means to be carbon negative, neutral or positive. Here are the definitions of the main climate action approaches:

CARBON NEUTRAL: You have not produced more carbon than you have sequestered. A tree is naturally carbon neutral.

CARBON NEGATIVE: You have drawn down more carbon than you have emitted.

CARBON POSITIVE: You have worked to create a net positive carbon scenario whereby you have drawn down more than you've created and invested in additional carbon reductions.

NET ZERO: The state of carbon neutrality is often called net zero, whereby GHG emissions drawdown to zero by removing or eliminating them entirely from society.

CARBON OFFSETTING: You invest in carbon capture to offset the emissions produced.

DECARBONIZATION: The process of removing carbon-emitting activities from a product, business and the economy.

Also, carbon is not the only bad guy when it comes to the greenhouse effect. Other climate-changing gases like methane and hydrofluorocarbons are released into the atmosphere as a result of all economic activities in varied forms.

Methane is released from agriculture, meat production and landfills. It's a 25x more potent GHG than carbon dioxide. Hydrofluorocarbons are often used in refrigerants and industrial processes.

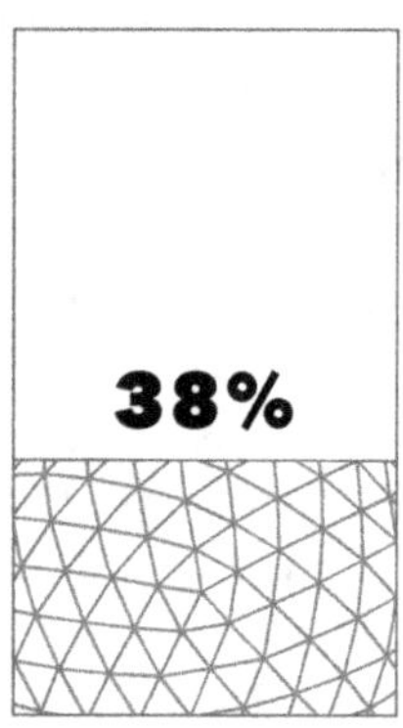

**FORTUNE 500 COMPANIES WITH
COMMITTED CLIMATE ACTIONS**

SOURCE: Source: Natural Capital Partners, Reality Check:
Climate Action and Commitments of the Fortune Global 500, 2021.

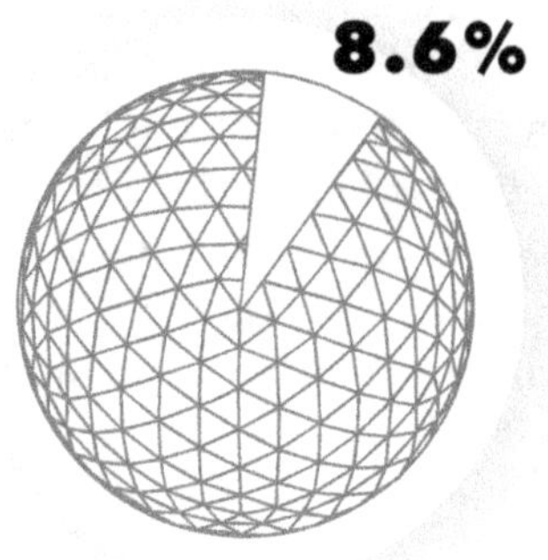

GLOBAL CIRCULARITY

SOURCE: Source: The Platform for Accelerating
the Circular Economy, Circular Gap Report 2021.

This is all to illustrate that addressing climate change is more complex than just reducing your energy consumption or paying for offsetting. It's about reconfiguring your company's operations, supply chains, procurement practices, materials and even your website design.

Some people conflate climate change and sustainability. Sustainability is the over-arching framework that climate change action fits within. Climate change is just one clear and obvious symptom of the flaws in our current linear economy — it is the outcome of a suffering system, where several interconnected systems became disrupted and damaged as a result of an imbalance.

Climate change affects all of us. It is not going away unless we take significant actions in the way the economy is designed and operates. We need multi-level and immediate actions from all sectors of society if we are to slow down the negative effects and ensure that we have a safe future to live in.

CLIMATE CHANGE AS A RISK FACTOR

The effects of climate change present significant risks for businesses. From crop failures to the mass migration of workers, there are many intersecting challenges resulting from the global effects of a changing climate.

There are already deep disruptions to supply chains, resource scarcity, infrastructure damage and worker shortages. On top of all that, sea level rise, land degradation, coastal erosion and freshwater contamination are all realities that we are now dealing with.

There is still time for action to reduce the more extreme predictions, and there are many interventions we can put in place to help us slow down the impacts and eventually reverse the negative effects of climate change. But this will take leadership, courage and conviction by all businesses to ensure that full systems changes are implemented.

Likewise, companies that avoid taking action or just do simplistic things will be penalized by customers and governments. It's still hard for many to see the need for change, especially those

Companies willing to go beyond the obvious and achieve change at multiple levels of operational activities, business model design and cultural change will see net positive results for the organization, the workforce and their customers — both now and into the future.

that have benefited from maintaining the current (polluting) status quo. That's why the next part of this guidebook is dedicated to cultural and organizational change.

THE GREENHOUSE GAS PROTOCOL

The Greenhouse Gas Protocol (ghgprotocol.org) is a set of standardized frameworks for measuring and managing emissions generated from public and private sector operations and supply chains.

The protocol sets out guidelines on how companies should measure and report on their emissions across three different scopes:

SCOPE 1 EMISSIONS: These are the direct emissions from sources that are owned or controlled by the organization. You have direct control over these, such as those released from a boiler in a factory or a fleet of vehicles you own.

- Measure the emissions directly created in facilities you own and operate.
- Take actions to reduce these through technological additions and behavioral change.

SCOPE 2 EMISSIONS: These are the indirect emissions created on behalf of the organization through the purchase of electricity, steam, heat and cooling from third parties. These GHG emissions include all operational energy for buildings or factories, as well as investments, leased assets and third party transportation.

- Whilst the GHG emissions are released by the third party, the demand is created by your organization's use, which means the impacts can be measured through energy audits.
- This is the easiest scope to address through efficiency measures such as reducing energy use and installing insulation, etc.

SCOPE 3 EMISSIONS: These are all the emissions from sources not owned or directly controlled by your organization, but related to your organization's activities.

These are all the GHG emissions that occur along the supply chain and are released on behalf of your organization by other parties in order for the company to operate.

- These can be considered as embodied impacts and apply to all external suppliers employed by the organization.

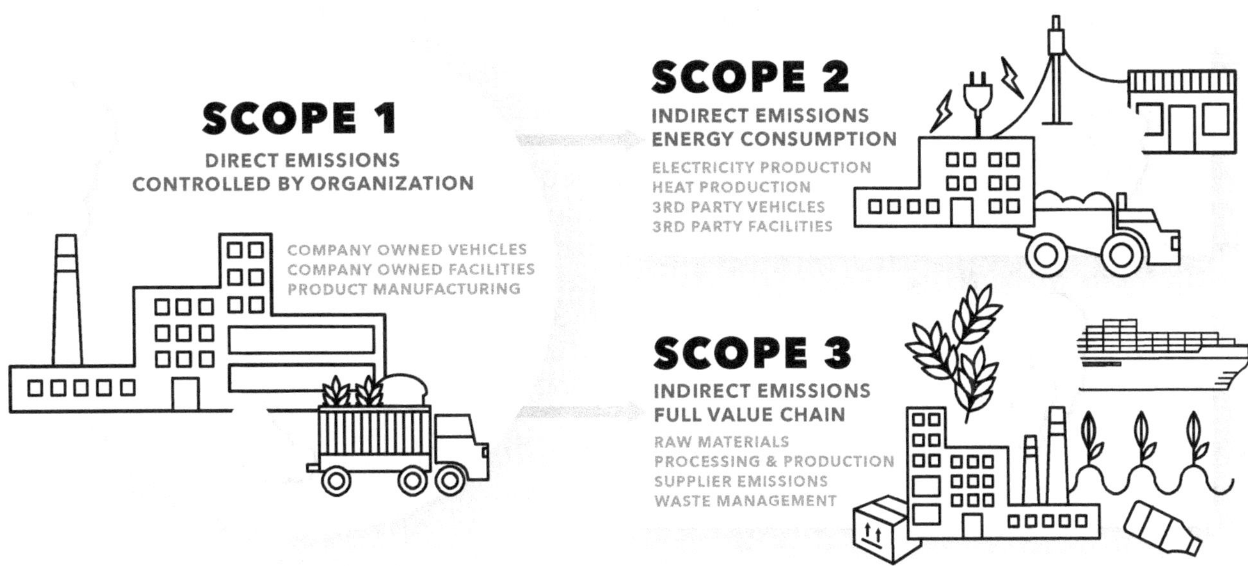

Adapted from: https://ghgprotocol.org

- Measure these through life cycle assessment, sustainable supply chains and environmental policies requiring third parties to report the GHGs.

Whilst Scopes 1 & 2 are mandatory to report on, Scope 3 is voluntary, but it's definitely where the most opportunity for transformative change lies. However, these impacts are often hidden in your products and supply chain processes, making it more complex to assess.

Thus it requires significant time and resource investment to detail what is occurring in your supply chain and then make changes to ensure your Scope 3 impacts are addressed (we dive into detailed ways of doing this in Part 3).

CARBON CONCEPT DEFINITIONS

CARBON ACCOUNTING: A process of auditing an organization's carbon emissions against the three categorized scopes and taking action to reduce or mitigate them.

CARBON FOOTPRINT: A tool to measure the total greenhouse gas emissions created by a company, product or individual.

CARBON CREDITS: A term used to describe any tradable permit that allows a company to emit a certain amount of greenhouse gases as part of a cap-and-trade system of pollution management.

CLIMATE BONDS: Green bonds, or climate bonds, are financial tools used to attempt to alter the market so that more sustainable investments are made. They are a type of fixed-income instrument intended to raise money for climate-positive, environmentally-beneficial projects.
CARBON DRAWDOWN: The process of drawing down GHGs from the atmosphere through sequestering processes, often utilizing natural systems to support this.

CARBON OFFSETTING: When companies pay to sequester carbon that they emit, such as by paying for trees to be planted or for geosequestration.

CARBON GEOSEQUESTRATION: A controversial approach to removing carbon from the atmosphere by pumping and storing it back underground into reservoirs made from the removal of other forms of fuels, such as natural gas.

WHAT'S THE WORLD DOING ABOUT CLIMATE CHANGE?

THE PARIS AGREEMENT: The international protocol signed by 187 countries in 2015 intended to reduce carbon emissions to limit global warming to 1.5°C by 2050. Countries under the agreement solidified climate proposals with formal approval, and must determine, plan and report on their climate change mitigation actions.

GOVERNMENT ACTIONS: Governments around the world have responded in different ways to their obligations to reduce carbon emissions under the Paris Agreement. From procurement policies through to heavy investment in renewables and nature-based solutions, a lot still needs to be done to decarbonize the economy.

CONFERENCE OF PARTIES (COP): Held annually, this UN conference is where all the signatories meet to discuss international legislations that need to be implemented to progress with the agreed actions to combat climate change.

SUSTAINABLE DEVELOPMENT GOALS (SDGS): A series of 17 goals set by the United Nations in 2015 to be achieved by 2030. Each lays out a pathway that, if addressed, will allow us to create a future that is more sustainable than today.

ORGANIZATIONAL ACTIONS: As a result of many different interventions, companies have also started to embrace the global shift toward sustainability and climate action. We are seeing leaders emerge around climate action and the circular economy in sectors such as apparel, consumer goods, and furniture.

Microsoft has committed to buying back all the carbon that they have emitted since starting in the 1970s. Ikea has committed to being net zero and 100% circular by 2050. Apple has a commitment of 100% carbon neutral for its supply chain and products by 2030.

ASSESSING THE TOP 10 CLIMATE ACTIONS

REFLECT

Before we get into the specifics of climate action, check your current actions against our Top 10 list of actions below.

GOAL

Establish a baseline for where you're currently at with taking climate action and set goals for activating more changes.

1-HOUR WORKSHOP IDEA

After checking your current actions, as a team, choose a few actions that you'd like to immediately address and make a plan to implement them.

TOP 10 CLIMATE ACTION CHECKLIST:

1. Switch organizational energy providers to ones that offer renewable sources.
2. Ask your financial service providers (like the bank or pension fund your company uses) what they invest in and swap to more ethical funds if needed.
3. Opt for electric transport options and incentivize employees to use them.
4. Take action to eliminate waste from your home, office and production processes.
5. Make products that last longer, and offer repair services to customers.
6. Become an active part of the circular economy.
7. Reduce your energy demands across your service and product life cycles.
8. Check your suppliers and switch to ones that are taking action to address climate change.
9. Share publicly what your organization is doing in order to help create momentum for change.
10. Switch to green servers and optimize your websites and apps with green code to be energy efficient and to reduce server and processing power.

☐ DATE COMPLETED ────────────────────

Small and medium businesses are also integrating circular economy initiatives, like Thousand Fell, who has started a take-back program for their recycled and sustainable material shoes. MUD Jeans has a leasing model and take-back program for their denim products. Loop Mission rescues fruit and produce from landfill to turn it into beer, juices, soap, gin, pet food and more.

The European Union has a significant commitment to transitioning to renewable energy, and the United States signed a progressive action plan in 2022.

POLLUTION AND WASTE

The world's soil, water and atmosphere have all been polluted by discharges from factories, industrial processes such as mining and waste in all its forms.

Waste is a lost resource. It's costly to citizens, as they must pay governments to cover the cost of waste removal, and it creates significant environmental and social issues in its disposal.

Waste is a negative impact of the current linear "take, make, waste" system, and it creates many of the environmental crises we face, like ocean plastic waste, methane emissions and heavy metal contamination. We produce over 2 billion tons of waste globally each year, with less than 20% being recycled (Kaza et al, 2018).

Because we produce so much waste, we have to go back to nature to get a new material to replace the wasted thing, which fuels ecosystem destruction.

In the last 70 years, we have moved from a more resource-conserving society to a disposable and single-use economy. This has placed a huge strain on the waste and recycling systems, resulting in many breaking under the pressure and pushing us into a global waste crisis.

For example, since 2018 China has refused to process other countries' trash, and many of the worlds' landfills and dumps are full. We are creating more and more complex materials that make recapturing more costly and dangerous, as in the case of electronic waste. Over 50 million tons of electronic waste are illegally trafficked around the world each year (WEF, 2019)!

CURRENT WASTE SYSTEMS

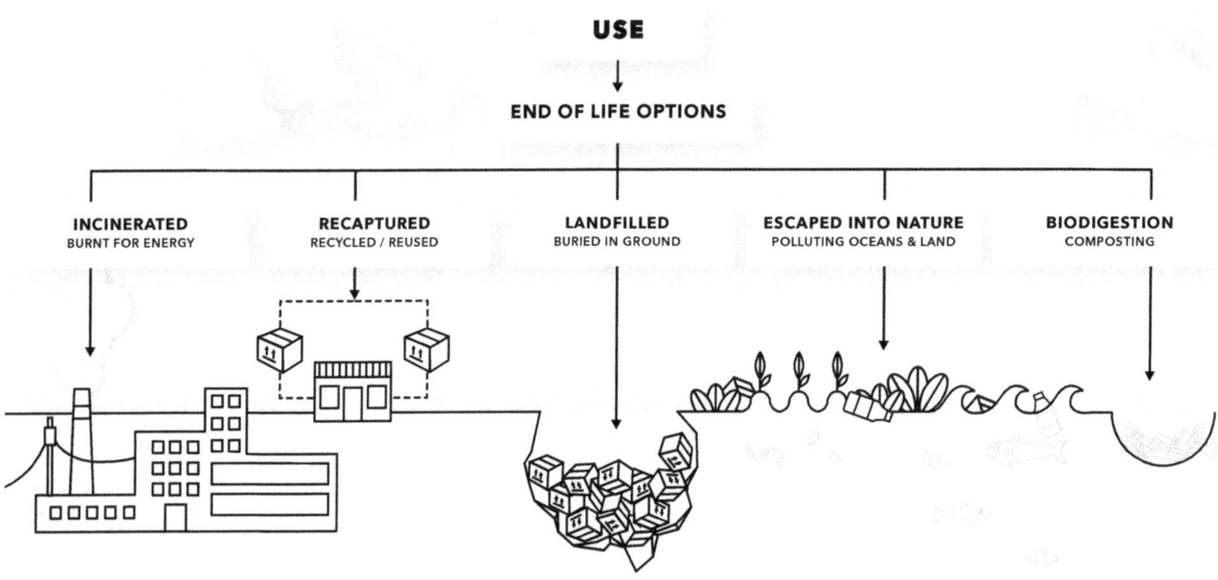

There are four main ways that solid waste is dealt with: landfills, incineration, recycling or escaping into nature.Additionally, biodigestion is a way of reusing organic materials.

Most produced waste is piled up in open dumps or buried in landfills where methane is produced. Leachates from all the liquids that mix together then escape out and contaminate the environment. Many modern landfills are designed to prevent leachates and to capture methane, but this is only when significant investment is made. Historical landfills all over the world continue to leach toxins into the environment.

In both open dumps and landfills, because so many complex materials are mixed together under airless environments, there are also issues with fires, which releases toxic gases into the atmosphere.

The alternative to landfill is incineration, which has losses and benefits. Incineration is about burning waste to make energy so it can replace fossil fuels. It turns waste into heat, flue gas and ash.

While some modern incinerators are used to generate electricity, others are simply designed to reduce the physical space that waste takes up, as burning trash can reduce solid waste by as much as 80%. Since all materials are burnt together, this means that they are lost forever. And although many modern incinerators are designed to avoid pollutants, they still can produce harmful particulate emissions.

Then there is recycling. In a perfect system, recapturing waste streams and reusing them in the most effective way would be an important part of the solution. But as it stands, recycling often just reinforces the problem because it psychologically enables individuals to use more single-use and disposable products. This results in a net environmental loss and significant increase in the use of raw materials. To put it in perspective, of all the plastic ever produced, only 9% has ever been recycled (OECD, 2022).

The final end of life option for waste generated is escaping into nature. This often occurs when it's expensive to manage waste or there's a lack of available options, thus driving littering or illegal dumping. There is a global issue with ocean plastic waste as a result of waste washing into rivers and oceans.

WISHCYCLING: The term used to describe the act of wishing that non-recyclable items were recyclable and thus placing them in the recycling bin, which then contaminates the entire batch of recycling and increases the cost of recycling for the processors.

ZERO WASTE: Not too long ago, terms like "zero waste" were boring policy directives thrown around by government departments with long-term strategies like "zero waste by 2020". But in the last few years, "going zero waste" and sustainable living in general have taken on an entirely cooler persona because of a lifestyle trend of young, hip Instagrammers and savvy YouTubers who are all helping to make zero waste a movement. In turn, they are also influencing product design and industry.

A zero waste lifestyler is someone who actively reduces their waste consumption by designing their life to combat acquiring wasteful things or products that will end up as trash, especially disposable and non-recyclable products and packaging.

LINEAR TO CIRCULAR ECONOMY

Currently the entire economy is based on extracting natural resources (take), processing these into usable goods (make) and then discarding them back into holes in the ground (waste). This is the linear economy, designed to produce waste and thus inherently unsustainable.

Under the linear model, we use double the resources that the Earth produces each year and then pump back more pollutants and byproducts than the Earth can absorb into the atmosphere, ground and water.

The alternative to this waste-based model is a circular economic system that intentionally cycles materials around the system, reusing before recycling and maintaining resources in different types of flows so they are not lost as waste. The goals of the circular economy are to eliminate waste entirely and to ensure that all production processes are regenerative. This is achieved by

LINEAR ECONOMY

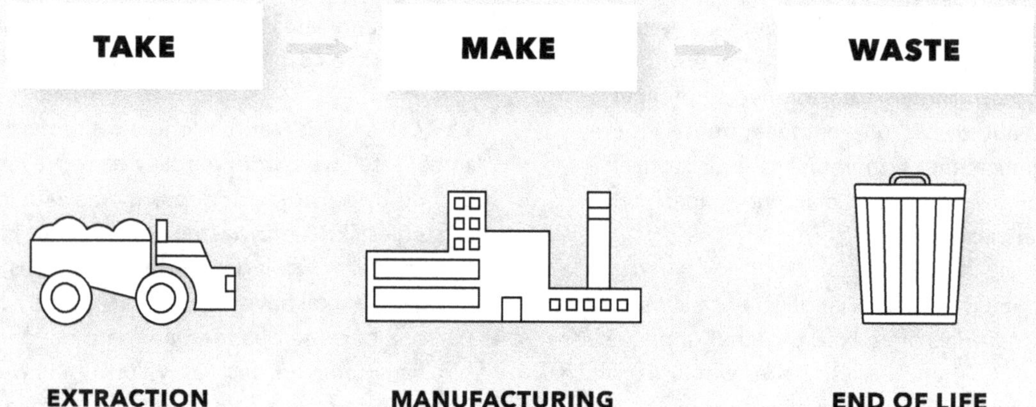

CIRCULAR ECONOMY

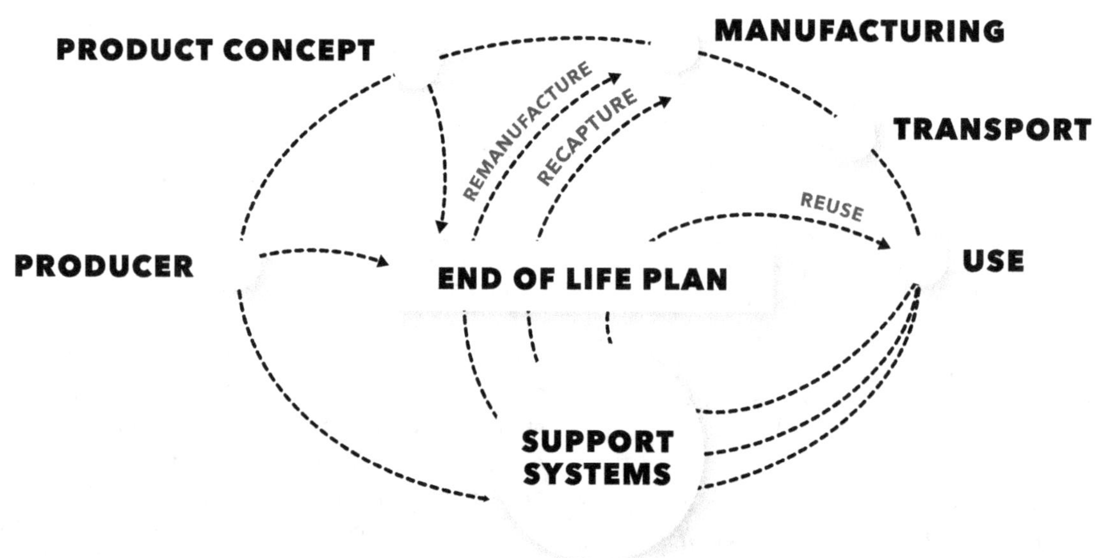

designing products and services so that they last longer and can be repaired or recaptured so as to not end up polluting the natural world or negatively impacting the systems that we need to sustain us.

Producers consider the full life of their products and take action to ensure that they are produced, delivered, used and recaptured in ways that restore rather than degrade the natural world.

In the circular economy, everything is designed to flow through systems that enable resources to be recaptured and repurposed. There are two main cycles:

> **"It's time to end the model of "take, make, break, and throw away' that is so harmful to our planet."**
>
> - EU Commissioner Frans Timmermans, 2022

BIOLOGICAL NUTRIENTS: Materials or stocks that can be easily absorbed or digested by natural systems in a benign way (eg: unbleached paper or food).

TECHNICAL NUTRIENTS: Materials or stocks that are manipulated by humans and cannot be easily re-integrated into nature (eg: plastics or technology). Goods are redesigned to cycle through these two main types of metabolism flows; instead of letting them pollute nature, we design products to be taken back and repurposed in environmentally-benign ways, through either cycle.

For example, all organic materials are biodigested to capture methane and use it as a power source; technological materials are designed for disassembly and sold as a service to ensure that they are recaptured.

New types of business models such as products as services are critical to this transformation; we explore these in more detail in Part 3.

CIRCULAR CREATION CYCLES

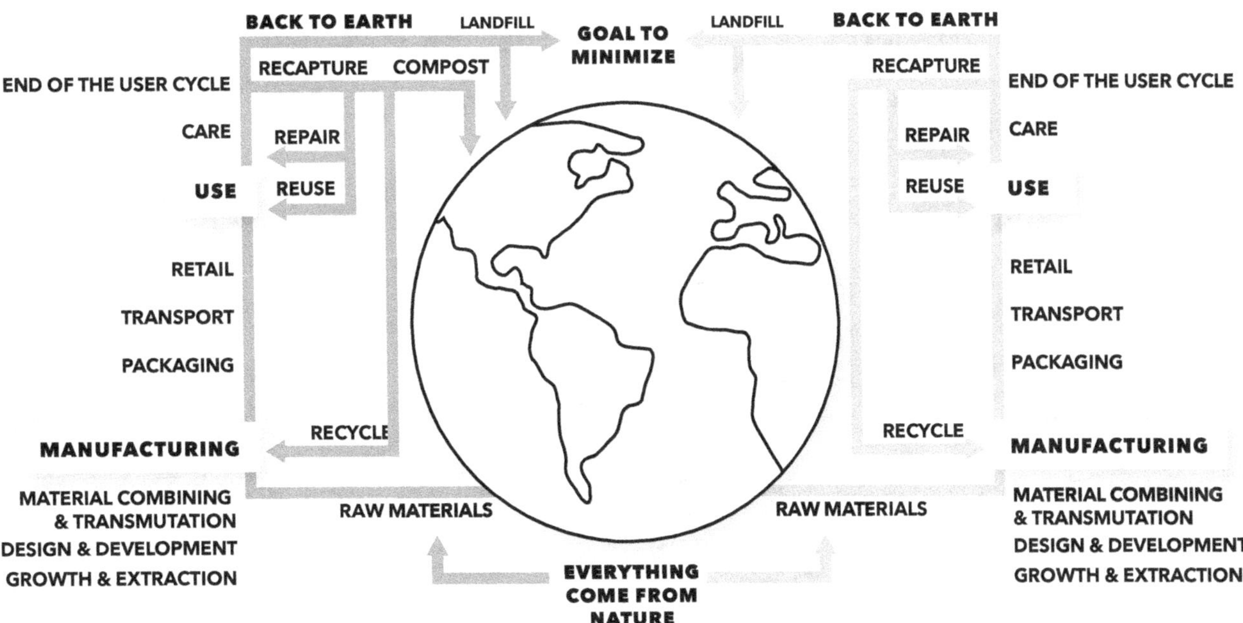

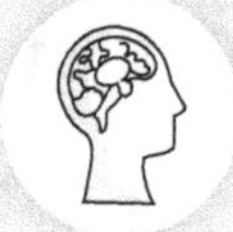

CONSIDERING CIRCULAR DESIGN AROUND US

REFLECT

Think about a circular system you've encountered as a consumer. What did you like/dislike about it? How would you improve it?

GOAL

Connect to real-world circular systems that you're personally familiar with and then consider what circular design looks like from a business perspective as you prepare to potentially make circular design decisions for your own organization.

1-HOUR WORKSHOP IDEA

Find 1 or 2 examples of circular design within your industry and discuss how they work.

Then, consider and discuss an aspect of your business that you could circularize.

Some examples: MUD Jeans, Loop by Unilever, Too Good To Go, Philips Light as a Service, Blueland, Sojo, ClubZero and Hello Tractor

☐ DATE COMPLETED ______________________________

DOUGHNUT ECONOMICS

Developed in 2012 by Oxford University economist Kate Raworth, The Doughnut Economy model offers a compass for sustainable development in the 21st century. It combines the social and planetary boundary concepts to form the shape of a donut.

The model has two concentric rings. The inner one is a social foundation that ensures no one is falling short on life's essentials (healthcare, education, equity, etc.). The second outer ring is an ecological ceiling that we must not exceed in order to ensure that humanity collectively stays within planetary boundaries.

These two sets of boundaries create a doughnut-shaped space that is ecologically safe and socially just: a space in which humanity can thrive.

The Doughnut presents an alternative to the growth-based economic model we currently adhere to and offers a model of development within the means of the planet that is equitable for all.

To find out more, visit the Doughnut Economics Lab (**www.doughnuteconomics.org**).

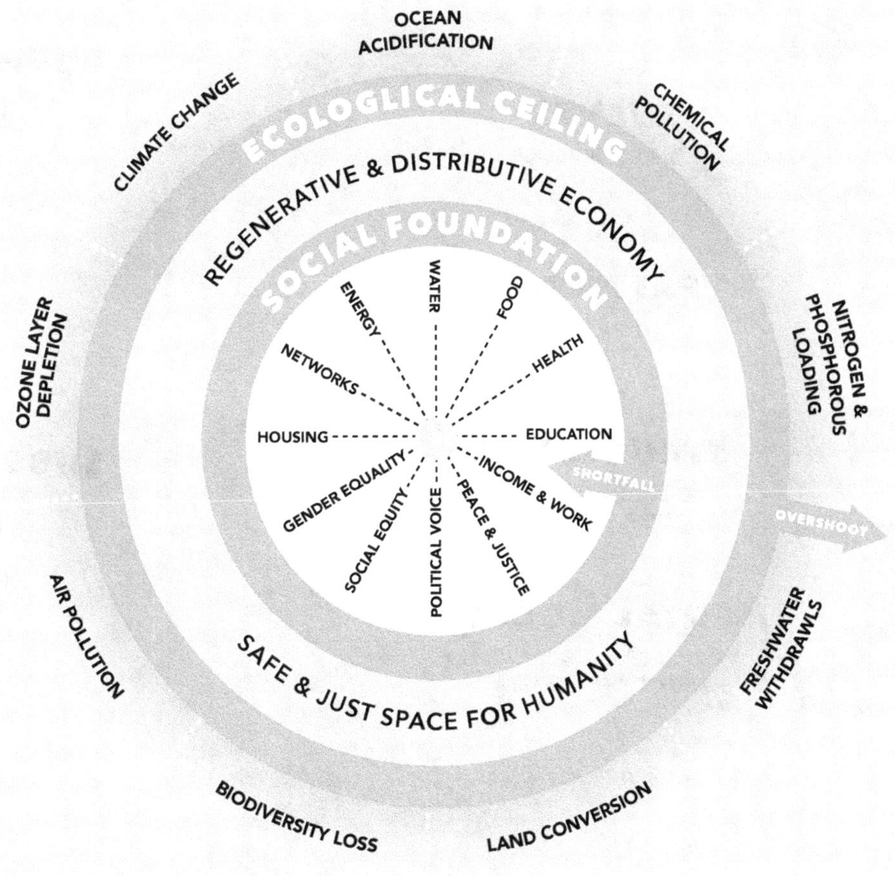

ADAPTED FROM: KATE RAWORTH, 2012

THINKING SHIFTS & TOOLS

Many of the social and environmental issues we face today are the product of solutions from the past; thus, the goal today is to design solutions that don't become tomorrow's problems.

To ensure that we don't repeat the same mistakes of the past or create new issues, we must change the way we see the world and our role within it.

This requires shifts in perspective, point of view and mindset by developing new ways of thinking and creating. One of the best tools for that is systems thinking.

In this section, we will explore how to move from linear to systems thinking in order to move beyond seeing only the most obvious part of the system, the tip of the iceberg, through to the substance hidden beneath. We'll also discuss the value shifts needed to create sustainability in business and society at large.

THE ICEBERG MODEL

ADAPTED FROM EDWARD T. HALL, 1976

TOP 12 SHIFTS IN THINKING FROM STATUS QUO TO FULL SYSTEMS SUSTAINABILITY

OLD APPROACH

NEW APPROACH

1 — Economic KPI tunnel vision → Equal consideration given to social and environmental impacts/improvements

2 — Short-term thinking → Long-term vision to ensure impacts don't negatively affect the future

3 — Siloed departments and thinking → Integrated, collaborative and networked systems, teams and thinking

4 — Impact avoidance → Impact acceptance and ownership for accountability

5 — Linear mindset → Circular processes and thinking

6 — Limited product responsibility → Full lifecycle product stewardship whereby the product is designed and managed by the producing agency across its entire life

7 — Selling products → Selling services with product components

8 — Planned obsolescence → Repair, remanufacture and upgrades as services that coexist with your products

9 — Paying to make a problem go away (such as carbon offsetting) → Seeing problems as opportunities for innovation and designing the problem away through better solutions

10 — Waste is part of the product life cycle → Waste is designed out right from the start of the design process

11 — Opaque supply chains → Fully transparent supply chains

12 — Avoiding social impacts → Equity and diversity as key drivers of business decisions

CONSIDERING NEW WAYS OF THINKING

REFLECT

Of the 12 thinking shifts, which 3 do you feel your organization could most immediately implement and improve?

GOAL

Begin priming your mindset for practical activation of the new ways of thinking that this guidebook presents.

1-HOUR WORKSHOP IDEA

Start the workshop by discussing your individual responses about which shifts to prioritize in order for your organization to move from the left to the right side of the spectrum.

Find the top 3 that you agree on as a team.

1. ____

2. ____

3. ____

Begin creating an internal campaign to share within the organization which thinking shifts you plan to implement first.

☐ DATE COMPLETED ___________________________

A SYSTEMS THINKING APPROACH

Systems thinking is about understanding the connections and relationships between things so that you can see how the world works. It's about flows, dynamics and interconnections.

A system is defined by the relationships between components that work together in a given environment in order to achieve a specific objective.

Systems thinking shifts how you see the world from lots of independent parts to a series of interconnected and interdependent systems that are emergent from the systems that they nest within.

As a mental tool, systems thinking seeks to oppose the reductionist worldview in which a system is measured and understood by the sum of its isolated parts, rather than its interconnected whole.

Reductionism is replaced with expansionism, meaning everything is part of a larger system and the connections between all elements are critical to maintaining the entire system. Everything is interconnected. Nothing can survive in isolation.

All biological systems are reliant upon something else for survival. Humans need food, air, and water to sustain our bodies, and trees need carbon dioxide and sunlight to thrive.

This is the same for the technical systems we have created; phones need electricity and cell service, cars need gas or power and buildings have sewage and water systems connected to them.

Many of the systems that make the planet and our lives function are invisible to us on a daily basis. Modern society's social systems require the industrial systems that we have created to form the physical world in which we live; both of these systems draw on the ecological systems that sustain life on Earth.

But many decisions are made in isolation of the systems that they work within. So, decisions made without consideration of the impacts that an action will have on another part of the system often create unintended consequences, or externalities.

This is basically what created the climate crisis: the continual contributions of greenhouse gases into the atmosphere at rates faster than the Earth's systems could sequester them has resulted in an imbalance

3 SYSTEMS AT PLAY

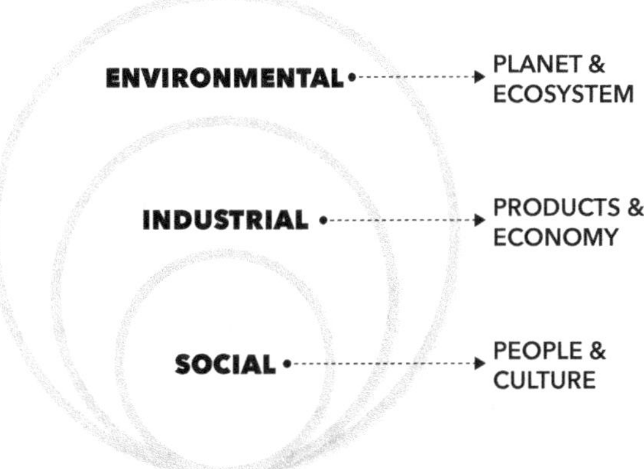

that has changed the weather systems, which in turn affects many other systems.

This is an example of a reinforcing feedback loop. There are two main types of feedbacks in systems dynamics; reinforcing (where elements of the system create more of the same, such as human population growth) and balancing (where parts of the system balance other parts out, like predators and prey).

Being able to see the full systems relationships and potential impacts right from the start of any decision-making process is critical to avoiding negative outcomes, or at least it allows for the mitigation of unavoidable impacts right from the start.

There are several tools used to explore systems dynamics. These include causal loop diagrams, systems archetypes and systems mapping.

SYSTEMS MAPPING

A system map is a visual representation of a system's relationships within a given boundary or scope. It's an important tool for integrating the dynamics and conditions that enable a phenomenon to exist.

The goal is to see the relationships and dynamics at play in the system you are working within and then use this full systems perspective to alter actions to create more beneficial outcomes.

You can use online tools to create systems maps from datasets (for example, kumu.io), or you can start with analog systems maps.

Hand-drawn analog maps are very useful because the act of creating them helps to identify the intricacies of the relationships and feedback loops. They are great as a collaboration tool and help to provide a snapshot of a complex system in real time.

Systems mapping is one of the key tools of a systems thinker. You identify and write down the elements or "things" within a system and then start to explore how they interconnect, relate and act within the bigger system you are exploring.

To get started, identify the system you want to explore, write down all the aspects you can anywhere on a page and then start to draw connections between them.

The page should get very messy, as you have a spaghetti-like maze of connections. From here, you can look for unique insights and discoveries to develop intervention points, status quo shifts or decisions that will dramatically change the system in the most effective way.

Ultimately, systems maps deepen your understanding of the system that you are working within, which is crucial because if you don't understand a system, then it's very hard to change it. To learn more about systems thinking, see our other handbooks and classes at online.unschools.co

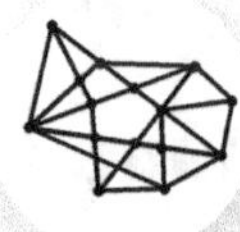

WHAT IS A SYSTEM?

To qualify as a system, it must be both dynamic (constantly changing) and evolving (having emergent properties).

It must be connected to elements, actors, agencies, nodes, stocks, the "parts" and have a boundary.

The edge of the universe is perhaps an exception to this, but we can still define a solar system by the boundaries of a constellation.

In many cases, when you take one part of the system away, it ceases to function, as in taking the wheels off a car or removing a vital organ from a human body.

Relationships are how system dynamics are formed. The outputs from one system are the inputs to another.

Nature is one of the best examples of interactive systems design — it is composed of many individual parts working together to create the dynamic whole that is the planet.

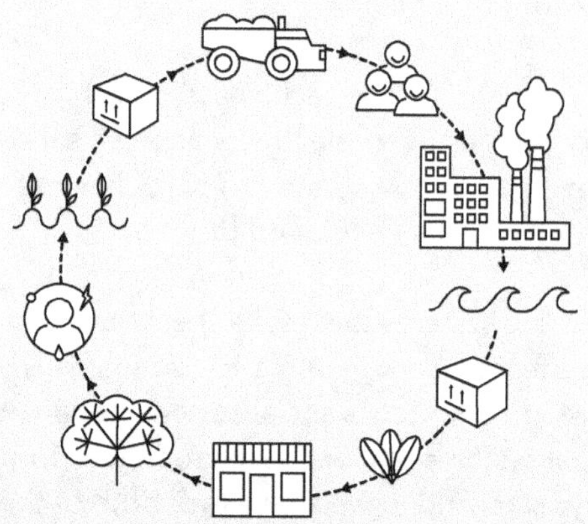

VALUE SHIFTS

In order to make any of the changes we are discussing in this guidebook, we must work toward a value shift in society and the economy, moving away from a growth-is-best mindset to a sustainable approach to gaining and transferring value.

This doesn't mean that we won't be able to meet our needs, innovate or create wealth; it means that we must find ways of doing these things within a constrained system (nature) and completely rewrite the code of conduct on creating waste.

The circular economy proposes eliminating waste from the system because it's a loss in value. The diagram below shows the circular economy cycles overlaid with the big-picture societal shifts that we need to embrace. If we don't cycle values as much as resources, then we will continue to create problems for the future today.

With a systems mindset and a value shift, we can foster a stronger understanding of the potential negative outcomes of our actions before we even take them, allowing far greater innovation and meeting societal needs in sustainable, regenerative ways.

CIRCULAR TRANSFORMATION VALUE MAP

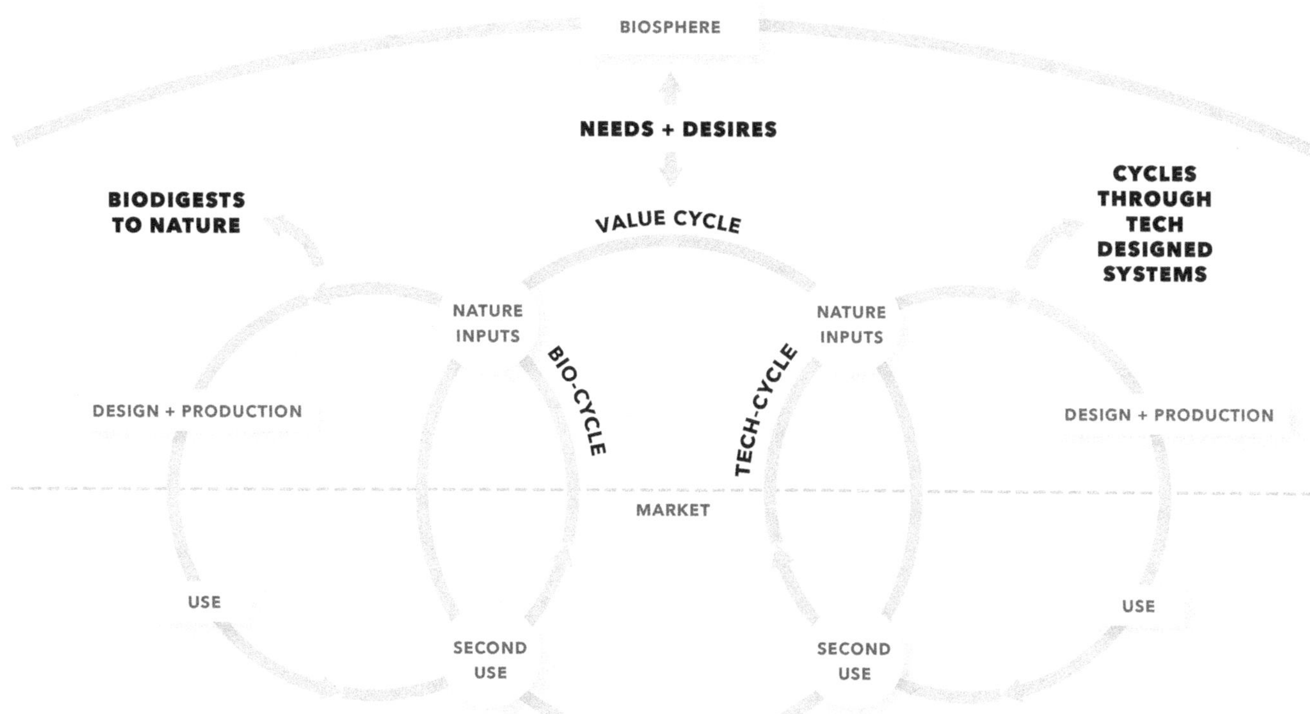

SYSTEMS THINKING SHIFTS

FROM	TO
DISCONNECTION	INTERCONNECTEDNESS
LINEAR	CIRCULAR
SILOS	EMERGENCE
PIECES	WHOLES
ANALYSIS	SYNTHESIS
ISOLATION	RELATIONSHIPS

REFLECTION ACTIVITY

SYSTEMS MAPPING

REFLECT

Think about a time that you realized two things were interconnected (for example, your cell phone is pointless if not charged or connected to a cell service, or you are reliant on oxygen for survival). What helped you make the discovery? Think of 3 other interconnected systems. Consider how they are dependent and what other systems they are connected to.

GOAL

Develop the capacity to rapidly see relationships and interconnectivity.

1-HOUR WORKSHOP IDEA

Practice systems mapping together! This is best suited for groups of 3-4 people but can be done individually as well.

To get started with analog systems mapping, grab a piece of paper and write a core theme or topic of exploration in the middle. Then throw down every "node" related to it anywhere on the page (this is not a mindmap, so don't make it linear!). A node is anything that is within the system.

There is nothing that won't fit in some way, so avoid editing yourself. Once your page is filled with nodes, start drawing connections between them and adding any new ideas that come to mind as you do that. Your page should look very messy.

Once it's filled with interconnected lines, you can take a bird's eye view to establish what the new insights are, which dynamics are occurring within this system and where you could potentially design interventions that will effect change.

☐ DATE COMPLETED ______________________________

LIFE CYCLE ASSESSMENT (LCA)

Absolutely everything that is created goes through a series of life cycle stages, from raw material extraction to end of life. The scientific process of understanding the impacts that occur as a result of the materials that move through our economy is called Life Cycle Assessment (LCA).

This enables a full picture perspective of where ecological impacts are occurring so that changes can be made to dramatically reduce and eliminate them. LCA is governed by an International Standard Organization (ISO) standard that helps ensure that published results are a robust and valid way of assessing the impacts of products in the economy.

LCA is a complex, detailed scientific process of breaking down all the inputs which go into making something exist and looking at the outputs that occur as a result.

In a life cycle assessment, the way materials flow through the economy in creating a product or service are measured against over 90 different impact categories that are linked to ecosystem health.

There are obvious categories (like carbon emissions and global warming potential) and lesser-known ones (such as eutrophication of waterways, human toxicity and ozone-depleting potential).

It's important to acknowledge that it is complicated and time consuming to do a full LCA, and in many cases, it's best left to the experts who can be hired in to support the assessment process.

Although it is by far one of the most effective tools we have for investigating the impacts that actions in the economy have on the planet, it also requires years of research and experience to be effective at conducting life cycle assessments.

It's important to note that only full LCAs that have been peer-reviewed and produced in accordance with the ISO guidelines should be published or used to make claims about environmental performance.

Another important thing to note about life cycle assessment is that it does not currently include social impact; however, there is an international community of experts exploring how social indicators and impact assessment can be integrated into the LCA methodology.

LIFE CYCLE THINKING (LCT)

From the scientific work done in LCAs, a more streamlined tool called Life Cycle Thinking (LCT) has

LIFE CYCLE STAGES

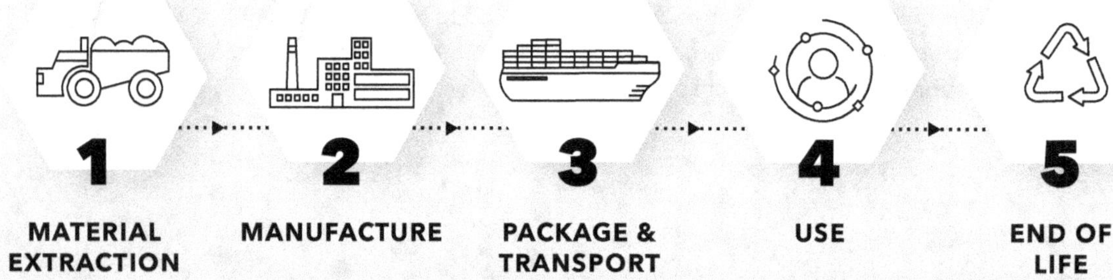

JUMP TO PAGE 112 IN PART 3 FOR A MORE DETAILED LOOK AT LIFE CYCLE THINKING

emerged. This is, in part, a mindset that explores the full life of a product or service (as opposed to just focusing on one area such as materials or end of life). It also encourages producers to think about the cause and effect of actions, along with the consequences of design and business decisions.

LCT is a decision support tool that expands the point of view from one dimension to the entire life of the product. It goes all the way back to the change of land for the extraction of raw materials. Next, it considers the manufacturing of raw materials and products, along with the packaging and transportation. Then, LCT analyzes the use phase and the future of end-of-life scenarios.

These life cycle stages are explored through life cycle mapping, a tool that helps you gain a full perspective of your product as it moves through the current linear economy. You'll learn how to do life cycle mapping in Part 3 of this guidebook.

Life cycle data is also used for the Type 3 Ecolabel called an Environmental Product Declaration. This is a publishable data sheet that helps other companies and consumers see the environmental performance of your product and is thus a desirable aspect of supply chain decision- making.

SUSTAINABILITY IN BUSINESS CONCEPT DEFINITIONS

Within the sustainability arena, there are many additional approaches from policy through to business that are important to know when developing your own strategies:

POLLUTER PAYS

A principle that is often applied to environmental law that determines that the polluter should pay for the clean up of the ecosystem that their actions damaged.

EXTENDED PRODUCER RESPONSIBILITY

A policy approach where the full life-cycle environmental costs associated with a product are added to the final sale price. This extra revenue is then used to manage the product stewardship.

PRODUCT STEWARDSHIP

The parent of the design, production and sales of a product takes responsibility for reducing the environmental impact of their product throughout its entire life cycle, ensuring that there are appropriate end-of-life options and that these are managed by the parent company.

CLEANER PRODUCTION

A preventative measure by companies to reduce the waste and pollution associated with the production of their goods.

SUSTAINABLE PROCUREMENT

Organizations seek out goods and services that have a reduced environmental impact through all aspects of the life cycle, avoid environmentally-damaging products and make changes to purchasing practices to support sustainability throughout the organization, as well as to create wider value chains.

TRUE COST ACCOUNTING

A type of accounting that takes into consideration the full externalities and costs associated with delivering a service, doing business or creating a product.

ESG: ENVIRONMENTAL, SOCIAL & GOVERNANCE

This is when investment decisions are made in accordance with the ESG factors, designed to encourage more investment in ethical and sustainable companies. There are ESG funds, and in the European Union, there is a regulation for financial institutions and publicly-listed companies to report ESG alignment.

BEWARE OF GREENWASHING AND GREEN MYTHS

A major trip hazard that organizations get caught up in when first trying to engage with sustainability is greenwashing and green myths. Greenwashing is when companies mislead consumers into thinking their products are greener than they actually are.

Oftentimes more money is invested in marketing their products as "green" rather than actually doing the work required to ensure that they are sustainable and can validate any environmental performance claims made.

Many organizations get caught up in greenwashing because they rely on green myths, which are the persistent ideas of what is sustainable, such as being made of a biodegradable material or being recyclable. These are simply properties of a material, not the defining factors of a product's sustainability. Green myths are perpetuated because there is a lack of core scientific and technical knowledge about what sustainability is and how it applies to your specific industry or product category.

While some greenwashing is unintentional, it can also be intentionally carried out through a wide range of marketing and PR efforts by companies who want economic rewards without having to do the work to get the actual green benefits — for example, putting a picture of a panda on their packaging or using popular terms like vegan, cruelty-free or eco-friendly.

To try to stop this, many countries now have legislation to protect consumers from misleading claims. As a general rule, if you can't measure it, you can't claim it. Be sure that products you are promoting or buying don't fall into the greenwashing trap and that the true benefits have been explored.

> **Greenwashing is defined as: "To make people believe that your company is doing more to protect the environment than it really is."**
>
> - Cambridge Dictionary

This is where tools such as the GHG Protocol and LCA are so crucial, as they provide the transparent and peer-reviewed data needed to validate claims. Another key way to leapfrog greenwashing issues is to invest in talent that has the technical skills to ensure you are making valid claims.

Reskill your existing workers to have a solid understanding of what sustainability is and what it is not (for example, give them this guidebook or have them take the swivelskills.com introductory training program).

GREENWASHING

Examples of High-Profile Greenwashing Cases:

- Volkswagen cheating the pollution emissions tests, 2015 (with over $20 Billion USD paid in fines and fees)
- Amazon advertising plastic products misleadingly labeled as "biodegradable" ($1.5 Million USD paid out in a settlement), 2018
- H&M's Conscious Collection having more synthetics than its normal range (72% as compared to 61%), 2021 (Lawsuit filed Aug. 2022)
- HSBC funding coal projects despite pledging to go carbon neutral, 2021
- Keurig promoting false claims of recyclability on their coffee pods, 2022 (Over $3 Million USD in settlements and fines)
- Ikea sourcing timber via illegal logging, 2021

Examples of Legislation Designed to Combat Greenwashing:

- **United Kingdom:** The Competition and Markets Authority (CMA) Green Claims Code, 2021
- **Australia:** The Competition and Consumer Act 2010 (also referred to as the Australian Consumer Law) provides legislation on environmental claims
- **European Union:** Substantiating Green Claims Legislation, 2019
- **United States:** Federal Trade Commission (FTC) Green Guides, last revised 2012
- **California, US:** Truth in Environmental Advertising, 2021

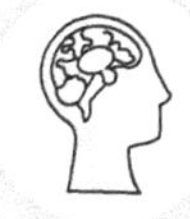

EXPLORING GREENWASHING

REFLECT

Do an online search for recent greenwashing cases in your industry.

For example, the fast fashion sector has recently had some high profile cases against them.

Use the greenwashing checklist on the following page to check to see where the examples you have found went wrong.

Explore if there are any greenwashing regulations that are relevant to your industry/product category.

GOAL

Learn how to spot greenwashing to help ensure that your organization does not participate in greenwashing.

1-HOUR WORKSHOP IDEA

Use the checklist on the next page to assess whether your company is participating in greenwashing. If so, list the actions you can take to rectify this.

☐ DATE COMPLETED ________________________________

GREENWASHING CHECKLIST

HIDING IMPACTS

☐ We have been clear and open about any potential trade-offs or hidden impacts.

☐ We have done the assessments, research and investigations to ensure that we don't have hidden impacts.

☐ We are not in any way trying to mislead our customers about potential impacts.

Fill in another hidden impact you've noticed in your industry to avoid:

____

____

MISLEADING CLAIMS

☐ We have not made any public claims that we can't back up with clear data and facts.

☐ We have checked to ensure that all our marketing materials are legitimate and not misleading in any way.

☐ We have not alluded to any relationships or product performance benefits that could be misinterpreted by customers.

Fill in another misleading claim you've noticed in your industry to avoid:

____

____

BEING VAGUE

☐ There are no vague or wishy-washy statements on our products or marketing about what we have done or will be doing.

☐ We have not said things like all natural, 100% recyclable or statements that don't really mean much.

☐ We have been open and transparent with our current and future actions.

Fill in another vague claim you've noticed in your industry to avoid:

____

____

FALSE OR UNVALIDATED LABELS

☐ We have not made up our own labels or pretended to have association with other labels.

☐ All labels we do have are legitimate and respected eco-labels.

☐ All images and icons we use are legitimate, true and 3rd-party validated.

Fill in another unvalidated claim or label you've noticed in your industry to avoid:

____

____

GREENWASHING CHECKLIST

INVESTED MORE IN MARKETING

- ☐ We have made sure that we have invested just as much or more in our sustainability R&D as our marketing spend to promote our green credentials.

- ☐ We have hired experts and are confident that what we are saying and doing is legitimate.

Fill in another area that you have invested in (skill training, assessments, etc.):

____

____

COMPARISONS

- ☐ We are not comparing ourselves to other products that have nothing to do with us.

- ☐ Any claims we do make against our competitors are legitimate, tested and can be validated.

- ☐ We are not confusing consumers by mentioning unrelated benefits (such as paraben free, etc.).

Fill in another comparison you've noticed in your industry to avoid:

____

____

MISLEADING WORDS AND/OR IMAGES

- ☐ We have been clear and open about any potential trade-offs or hidden impacts.

- ☐ We have checked all the images and icons that we are using to make sure that they don't create any misleading associations.

- ☐ We have not made any claims that make it sound like we are better than we actually are.

Fill in another way that you have ensured transparency & clarity in your communications:

____

____

GOOD BY ASSOCIATION

- ☐ We have not just done some small act that makes us look good to get associated credit.

- ☐ All our stakeholders, suppliers, collaborators, etc. are also working to avoid greenwashing.

- ☐ We are not using environmental organizations on our branding or packaging to make us look good.

Fill in another way you have gone deeper than just small and surface level claims:

____

____

GREEN MYTHS

Green myths are false but persistent ideas about what is/is not sustainable or beneficial from a social and environmental perspective. An example would be the idea that paper is an "eco-friendly" material and plastic is not.

Remember that many persistent green myths describe the properties of a material. Terms like biodegradable, recyclable and renewable are nice, easy phrases that sound good, but they don't tell you much about the product's true environmental impact. They look only at end of life and describe a best-case scenario where the product is disposed of responsibly.

Avoiding the buzzwords is also a good place to start when you're dealing with green myths. Look behind the labels and make sure that the products are truly sustainable.

3 PERSISTENT GREEN MYTHS

BIODEGRADABILITY IS BEST: Terms like biodegradable, recyclable and renewable are used interchangeably to insinuate they're good for the planet. These words simply describe a material's property, not an environmental benefit, and they represent a best-case disposal scenario.

PAPER VS PLASTIC: True sustainability can only be understood from a full life cycle, systems-based perspective. In the case of paper vs plastic, in countless life cycle assessments from the past 20 years, plastic shopping bags scored better than their paper counterparts — and even more so than the recycled paper option! Why? Because paper weighs 4-10x more and contains up to 10x more materials that require extraction from nature, which are then processed, shipped and eventually discarded. The place where plastic scores worse is in disposability, which is why we encourage going post-disposable where possible.

RECYCLING IS GREAT: We are now coming to understand that recycling can create a negative rebound effect whereby recycling validates disposability. It's a placebo solution to the complex waste crisis we have caused. The things you are separating and putting in your recycling bins are probably not being recycled — and there's a good chance that they are ending up somewhere you never imagined. This means that we are increasing the amount of disposable products being produced, used and discarded, as well as requiring more natural materials to be extracted to cope with the demand. The net result is more "stuff" being produced and with it, more waste.

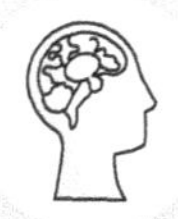

REFLECTION ACTIVITY

PART 1 RECAP

1 What reservations or preconceived ideas do you have about the concept and application of social and environmental change?

2 In what ways does embracing sustainability feel like an opportunity for you?

3 What externalities does your business contribute to?

4 What steps have been taken to address them?

5 How can valuing nature help create a mindset shift in your organization, and how can you make the value of nature tangible for your team?

6 What does being a climate action leader look like for your organization?

7 How can you invest in expanding your organization's systems thinking abilities?

8 What are three strategies you can adopt to ensure that your organization is not greenwashing?

☐ DATE COMPLETED ________________________

PART 2

ORGANIZATIONAL CHANGE

Sustainability is all about transformation and change; those who are resistant to change are often left behind as the transformation takes hold.

I love telling this story of the horse and cart industry to CEOs and leaders who are resistant to adopt sustainability wholly within their business, as it reminds us all of the need to push past our own limiting thoughts and biases to see around the corners of the future.

In the 1910s, a few years after Ford released his Model T automobile (which would go on to become the fastest selling automobile of the time), the head of the horse and cart Industry Association stood up at their annual conference in New York to address a crowd of concerned peers.

He said, "Make no mistake my friends! The horse and cart industry is here to stay. It's not like they can put a fuel station on every corner."

Within five years, their horse and cart industry was dead.

Change is about adapting and being willing to abandon one horse for another when it's tired and no longer fit for the purpose.

2.1 A FUTURE-POSITIVE APPROACH

Taking action to address the environmental and social impacts of your company is not just about responding to growing market trends, nor is it just about ensuring that you are operating in ethical and responsible ways.

These should already be core aspects of your business, but sustainability is about having foresight and being future ready now. By seeing the opportunities that big challenges and disruptions create and being willing to adapt (rather than maintain the status quo), you can create a positive culture around approaching sustainability, all whilst growing your business, creating value, and retaining excellent workers.

The beauty in this future-positive approach is that foresight allows for sustainability to be integrated into all aspects of operations and product delivery. From the design of business models, products and services through to sustainability-centric policies, you can transition from being a linear company to a circular one in a progressive and positive way.

BEING AN INTRAPRENEUR

This is someone within an organization (usually an employee or leader) who develops innovative ideas, projects or changes that help the company grow. Since an intrapreneur is inside the company, they can develop new ways of doing things with a deeper knowledge of how the company already operates. Thus, they can help leverage changes based on the organizational culture, which will in turn help enhance the company's future.

Change requires leadership from governments, CEOs, creative thinkers and intrapreneurs. In this section we will explore modes of making change and the tools needed to positively shift organizational culture toward full-systems sustainability. Any change approach will inevitably encounter barriers and resistance, so we'll be covering a selection of tools that you can employ to pre-empt and circumnavigate this ahead of time in order to develop an effective future-positive transformation strategy.

2.2 CULTURES OF CHANGE

Change is all about transformation.

Therefore, to make change is to facilitate transformational experiences that move from one state to another. But change is also constant, and at times, unpredictable.

Sustainability is also about change — changes to the way businesses operate, the product designs, value chain relationships, material choices, business models, company culture and customer engagement.

At the base of any physical and material changes is cultural change, which influences mindsets and behaviors.

To be successful in transitioning away from the linear business-as-usual model (discussed on page 47) to a more sustainable and circular one, you must start with shifting organizational culture so that your company has strong values that permeate throughout the organization.

Innovation is also all about change, and the companies that embrace a dynamic culture focused on transformation benefit from their own self disruption.

From a systems perspective, change is dynamic. Each change that's made, in turn, changes the other aspects of the world, and ultimately, micro changes add up to have bigger impacts on the planet through the things that we choose to do (or not to do). Thus, actions add up to impacts both as individuals and as members of an organization. That's the power of intentionally creating positive change and taking purposeful actions to transform away from unsustainable actions.

"The secret of change is to focus all of your energy not on fighting the old, but on building the new."
- Socrates

IS CHANGE HARD?

People often declare that change is hard when they want to avoid doing something or when they feel threatened by the changes happening around them, usually as they are not seeing the immediate change that they desire or because they are fearful of what the change will bring.

In 500 BC, the Greek philosopher Heraclitus talked about change as a "universal flux." He said, "The only constant in life is change," and, "Stability is an illusion." If change is constant as Heraclitus said, then it is also chaotic — "an inescapable paradox, yet a beautiful necessity, critical to all life."

Rigidity and inflexible thinking makes things challenging. It causes an issue when people get stuck in thinking paradigms despite the world changing around them.

Although change is constant, it's in our human nature to experience resistance when change happens.

As you begin to apply new frames in your organization to create different processes and enact full systems sustainability, you'll inevitably encounter people who are not on board, whether they're people who want to maintain the status quo or those who resist the fact that customers want more sustainable products and ethical companies.

So, before blazing into organizational transformation, it's valuable to uncover the pre-existing perceptions as well as the cognitive biases and cultural barriers that limit change. This way you can start by planning ahead for how you can help your organization overcome barriers and grow together toward a better way of operating.

Depending on where you are in your organization's hierarchy, you may also experience resistance from the top. Power is obviously a major factor when designing a change process. Identifying your sphere of influence and creating a plan for activating more of your agency will enable you to effectively apply the strategies and tactics outlined in this guidebook.

AGENCY: Your capacity to exert power through an action or intervention that produces a particular effect. A personal awareness of your ability to exert influence on the world.

SPHERE OF INFLUENCE: Your ability to affect change grows based on your efforts to expand your skills, capabilities and experiences in making change; it's connected to the networks and community you speak to and interact with.

All ships need a captain to navigate them across the ocean, and this is the same for organizational change. Someone needs to have the foresight, courage and commitment to traverse unknown waters and move the company from the current state to another.

Strategic or corporate foresight is an approach to leadership that is action-oriented and future-focused. Rather than reacting to external pressures like regulations, customer demands or stakeholder pressure, leaders envision a better future scenario for their company and design a process of change that moves the ship to that destination.

Sustainability is part of the future for all companies — there is no way to avoid the need for every aspect of society to respect and work within the parameters of nature. So, how can you envision future operational and product delivery systems that integrate sustainability into the DNA of your organization?

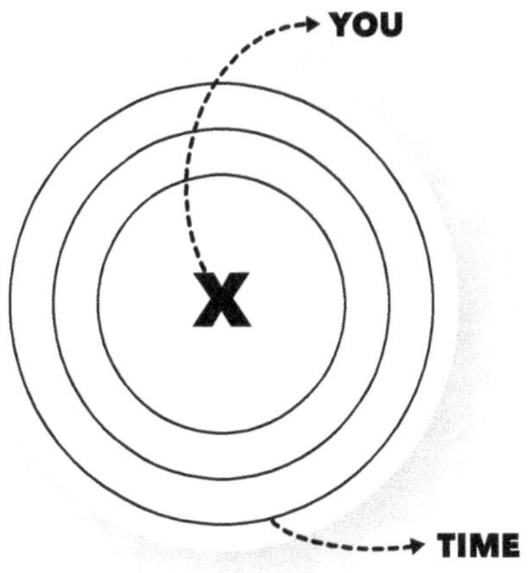

SPHERE OF INFLUENCE

HOW DOES YOUR ORGANIZATION HANDLE CHANGE?

REFLECT

Think about the current culture of change within your organization. On a scale of 1-10, 1 being most resistant and 10 being most open, how would you rate your organization's willingness to embrace change? Consider why this is the case and what you could do or see happening that would help shift this.

GOAL

Understand the baseline of where your company currently stands with change approaches to better prepare you to understand the complexities and barriers associated with transformation.

1-HOUR WORKSHOP IDEA

Develop a change action plan that identifies both any potential bottlenecks that you may experience based on your organizational culture as well as the bright spots, which are the aspects of your company that will enable change to progress. Consider these prompts:

- What changes have we successfully implemented in the past and why did they work?

- Who has the power and influence within the organization to lead the change journey?

- Where are the bottlenecks that would limit our change agenda?

- Why is (insert change goal) perceived as being hard/difficult/unattractive within our particular workplace culture?

- How can we design a change experience that is delightful and accessible to all without our organization?

☐ DATE COMPLETED ___________________________

2.3 HUMAN NATURE AND BARRIERS TO CHANGE

To better overcome resistance to organizational change, it's important to have a baseline understanding of why humans get uncomfortable with change. Here we'll explore some high-level concepts related to social norms, biases, the status quo and human habits before diving into how to identify and overcome the unique challenges your organization may face when embracing a change toward sustainability.

SOCIAL NORMS: Informal understandings of "appropriate" social behaviors that subtly govern our lives and societies. Norms differ from place to place, but they have similar impacts by providing the social cues of what is expected and rewarded in a person's behavior in order for them to fit in with that community or society.

These are things like, if and what kind of cutlery you use to eat, how you greet a stranger or whether you take your shoes off as soon as you walk into someone's house. Social norms can be explicit (obvious) or implicit (unspoken), and they often transfer between people in subtle ways through social cues of what is deemed appropriate or not.

Social norms are often pervasive and work to control or change culture because we have an innate desire to be socially accepted by those around us; thus, we replicate the status quo in order to fit in.

This plays out in company culture as well. If it's deemed okay to make jokes about exploitation in the supply chain, or if the social norm is to ensure that ethics is built into every decision — these can all be seeded and encouraged by good policies and practices, as well as leaders and the agents that exist within the community.

SOCIAL CONTAGION: Richard Dawkins is the author of the book "The Selfish Gene".It first proposed the idea of a meme in 1976, before internet culture took it on. Dawkins proposed that social contagion is like a virus that infects people. We "catch" ideas and behaviors from each other, which results in the rapid uptake of certain trends and the disregard of others — as well as how we see social change happen in any direction, be it desirable or not.

Since we are influenced by others around us, we learn how to reinforce what has come before from the people we interact with; unless we actively challenge what we are taught, we become the replicators of the status quo (Giddens, 1984). This is how unsustainability gets embedded into company

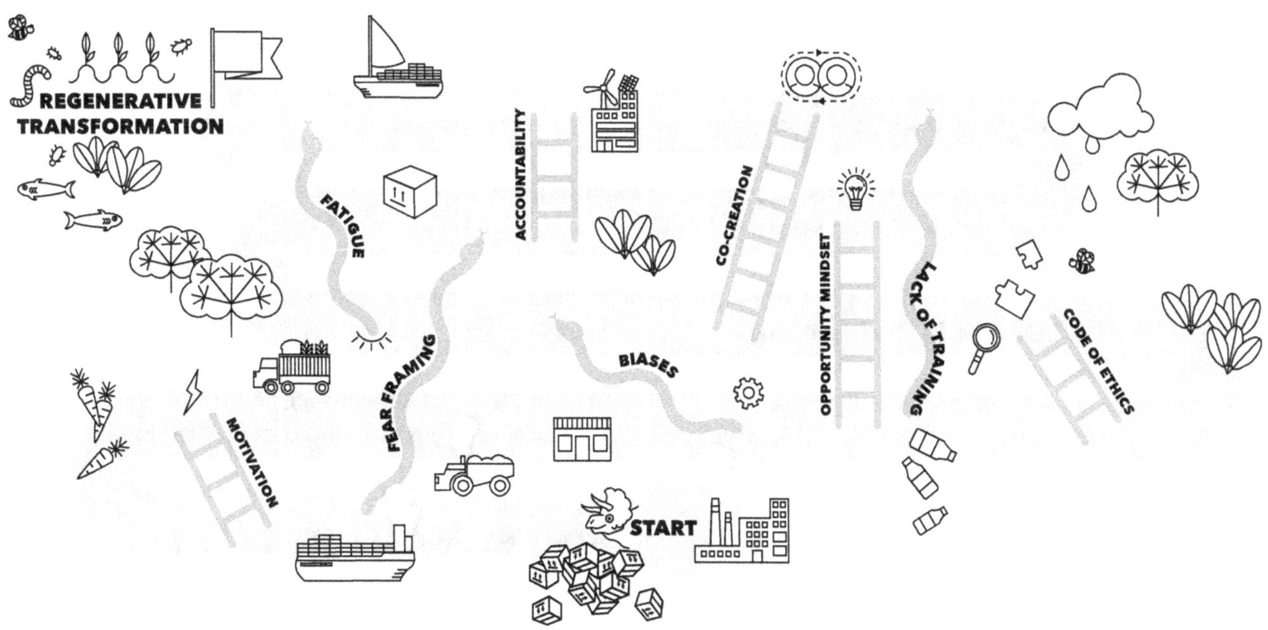

culture (and society), as we "catch" and replicate social norms.

Reflect on any unsustainable cultural norms that exist within you organization. How have they been replicated over time, and what changes would work to challenge them effectively?

COGNITIVE BIAS: Biases are mistakes in reasoning and cognitive decision making. We all have them, and there are hundreds of cognitive biases that affect us in very similar ways. From confirmation bias (where we seek out information that reinforces what we already believe) to optimism bias (where we believe that bad things don't happen to us specifically) through to sunk cost (where it's hard for us to give up on something we have invested in), these shared neurological faults greatly affect our willingness to accept new information, embrace diversity or make change.

Being willing to challenge and rewrite organizational norms is one of the cornerstones of creating a successful sustainability change initiative.

STATUS QUO BIAS: One downside of the norm-seeking aspect of human behavior is a propensity toward sameness over diversity, resulting in a status quo bias, which is a desire to maintain the current state at all costs. This is often one of the major barriers to change within organizations. Those that have benefitted from maintaining the status quo are often those who have the power to ignite change; thus, they need to overcome their own bias to help facilitate change.

COGNITIVE DISSONANCE: This is another neurological issue that we all share, whereby there is a gap between what we say we will do and what we think we will do in a given situation. Dissonance is often experienced as a discomfort when two modes of thought or values are confronted and contradict each other. We want to feel consistency in our beliefs, so when cognitive dissonance is experienced, people often change their opinions instead of their behaviors to avoid the discomfort.

NEUROCHEMICAL REWARDS: The human brain is wired to secrete a cocktail of chemicals that motivate or alter behaviors. Positive rewards chemicals include serotonin, dopamine and oxytocin. The stress hormone is cortisol. Different neurochemicals affect us in different ways, but generally we are rewarded for replicating social norms, whereas stress is triggered when we are outside of cultural conventions.

HUMAN HABITS

In daily life, we all perform habits. These are the deep-rooted routines that make life easier and more efficient for us. From the field of psychology, habits are actions that are prompted by contexts that occur automatically. These are often learned through previous experiences and operate almost on autopilot.

Charles Duhigg wrote an excellent book called "The Power of Habit" (2012) that looks at the science of how habits form and can be changed. Duhigg describes what he calls the habit loop, whereby behaviors are reinforced through repetitive actions to create routines. The habit loop involves a cue that is reinforced via routine and solidified as a habit through reward — often a little rush of a neurochemical like dopamine or serotonin.

In order to break a habit, one has to rewrite the code that created it.

Behaviors are only one indicator of change. Most behaviors are in response to social norms and cultural conventions, so to change behaviors, we have to shift culture.

Identifying why some ideas, trends or actions catch on and become new norms is where we open up the space for significant and transformative change.

To summarize, changing social norms often requires challenging habits, and the best way to do that is to change the culture.

FORCES THAT LIMIT CHANGE

Over the years of working to effect change toward sustainability, I have identified three major forces

THE 3 F'S THAT LIMIT CHANGE

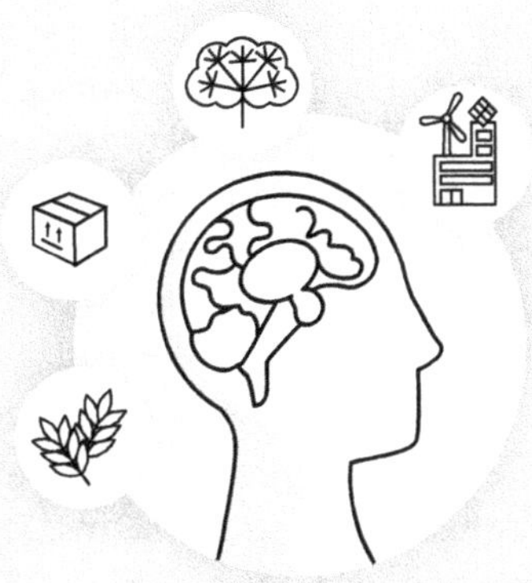

FRAMING

The historical idea that sustainability (in all its forms) is an optional add-on, something that is nice to have or only for tree-hugging hippies excludes many people from participating in it and justifies inaction. Instead, framing sustainability as both an opportunity for innovation as well as a critical part of all that we create and do challenges outdated ideas of who and why we should embrace it in all its forms.

FEAR

The great cognitive and creative restrictive force we all encounter at times is fear. Whether it's fear of the unknown or of a future that is filled with even greater challenges, fear of admitting you have been wrong or accepting that you need to change, fear results in avoidance and inaction (even denial) for many people. Climate change is a strong example of how fear can induce anxiety and inhibit change efforts. Fear should be confronted by realizing all problems hold their own solutions and that the future is defined by our actions today. Fear is often also remedied by action!

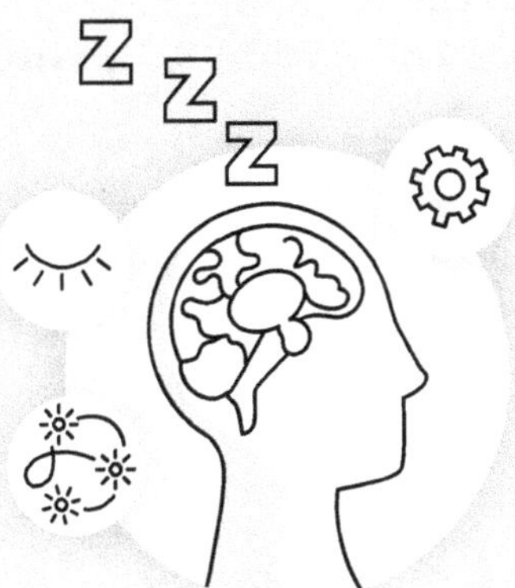

FATIGUE

It's exhausting to constantly try to make change when forces around you work to maintain the status quo. So, fatigue sets in and good intentions erode then turn into cynicism. Fatigue can be combatted by seeking out the bright spots in a system and then building a broader systems mindset. There is no blame in a constantly evolving system, and it's up to each of us to take part in designing the future we want to live in.

that limit change within an organization: framing, fear and fatigue.

By reflecting and identifying if and how these three F's affect you and your organization, you can design ways to overcome them.

FRAMING

Humans think in unconscious structures called frames to help interpret the world around them. They are a bundle of associations that can be evoked or pulled out of your brain's filing cabinet through language. Once triggered, the associations create a framed lens through which you see the world or interpret information.

George Lakoff is a cognitive linguist and philosopher who wrote a seminal handbook on framing called "Don't Think of an Elephant!" (2004). He explains how frames shape perception and that political leaders and mass communicators use frames to create moral panics by evoking emotional reactions through the use of metaphors that help coerce society.

Lakoff also explains issues with how we frame the environment when it comes to climate change: "... Environmental frames are the (typically unconscious) conceptual structures that people have in their brain circuitry to understand environmental issues. Frames are communicated via language and visual imagery. The right language is absolutely necessary for communicating 'the real crisis'. However, most people do not have the overall background system of frames needed to understand 'the real crisis'; simply providing a few words and slogans can at best help a very little," (Lakoff, 2010).

Frames often limit the way someone perceives something, as the brain subconsciously evokes frames, which come in connected systems. Thus, when we encounter an idea, term, concept, etc., we not only get the defining frame, but we also get the entire system that connects to that frame — i.e. when someone hears the word "environment" or "sustainability", it evokes the immediate mental reference that person holds (which may be positive or negative, and often involves recycling, eco-friendly, tree-hugging, etc.). This will draw on all the associated concepts and images the person has absorbed over time that are connected to the main frame.

HABIT FORMATION LOOP

ADAPTED FROM CHARLES DUHIGG, 2012

Frames can unite and divide people, create action or result in avoidance. Connected to social norms and biases, they can exist in our thoughts, in our interpersonal communication and in political/mass media communication.

Frames also draw on our schemas. A cognitive method of structuring and organizing information that creates patterns of thought assigned to parts of the world to help make sense of it; schemas are often evoked through language.

To add an additional layer to this, frames are connected to the emotional center of the brain, so a frame will also draw an emotional response (even if mild) and cloud the way someone perceives the issue being discussed.

For the last few decades, environmental issues have often been communicated through negative, fear-inducing or fluffy feel-good ways. As a result, many of the frames people hold today about the environment, sustainability and social issues draw on negative or outdated ideas about "doing the right thing". This is especially true in relation to business. When triggered, they can have the counterproductive effect of limiting interest, and thus, reducing creativity and motivation toward engaging and addressing the issues (Nisbet, 2009).

FEAR

Fear kicks into gear to protect us from perceived threats, which is why it's such a powerful tool often leveraged by politicians. Fear is part of our evolutionary defense system. Triggered by perceived threats, fear can often be irrational.

Fear can be a nagging or gripping thing; it eats away at us or strikes us with such intensity that we jump from our chairs, scream or run for our lives. It's an incredibly effective motivator to get us to avoid the things we don't want to deal with. If you are terrified of public speaking, then I bet you avoid a stage.

We avoid things that make us feel bad, and fear triggers the stress hormone cortisol. Fears have different effects on us — they can paralyze us or ignite a fire inside that drives us to take action.

FEAR-BASED MANIPULATION: Fear is often effectively leveraged to get support for politically-motivated acts like wars or public policy implementation. Moral panics are sometimes used to activate a sense of urgency. Fear is also an easy, well-trodden target for marketers and spin doctors. All humans are cognitively wired for personal and in-group survival, so issuing threats against us and our clan helps to either motivate or disable action, depending on the way the messages trigger your particular neurological reactions.

The content used to communicate climate change is steeped in a kind of fear that often turns to denial.

Even people who would say they believe in climate change have a nifty little set of unconscious brain tricks that reinforce a lack of urgency for action. There are two things playing out here: optimism bias and solutions aversion.

OPTIMISM BIAS: The safety net our brains need to get by each and every day of our lives; it's the "everything is going to be just fine" switch that we flick on when a fearful fact is encountered.

The brain goes to great cognitive lengths to craft a narrative of self-preservation so that your future will be fine. Thinking something like, "I have got this under control. It might be bad, but it won't be that bad for me," helps to alleviate the stress hormone cortisol that is triggered by fear. If we didn't have these types of brain tricks, none of us would get in airplanes after one crashes!

SOLUTIONS AVERSION: A fascinating case of brain trickery where people opt out of believing in a proposed solution when the solution does not affirm their current ideological perspective.

To add to this cocktail of subconscious brain biases playing out, there is another bias called the Dunning-Kruger Effect. It's named after the two behavioral economists who uncovered it, and it states that people never actually know what they don't know because people who don't know something often rate themselves higher on aptitude of that arena than those who do actually have knowledge on it. Thus, they avoid exposing themselves to the information that would allow them to gain knowledge to know what they didn't know before!

Deniers have a set of neurological hiccups working to prevent acquiring new information that would support the changes needed to contribute to solving the problem.

FATIGUE

It can be exhausting having to learn new things, battle overwhelming power structures or cycle through countless rounds of innovations.

Fatigue often plays out as a limiting force in transformation of a sustainable business because there is one person or a small group tasked with turning an incredibly large ship around. They are often under-resourced, sidelined or given hugely complex tasks within tight time frames.
When someone is fatigued, their ability to think creatively and divergently is limited. Likewise, their focus and decision-making are much harder, and in general, motivation and participation dwindles.

Fatigue can come about as a result of physical or mental exhaustion. It can make people easily irritated or frustrated. When fatigued due to overwork or over exposure to a topic that is cognitively difficult to comprehend, there is likely to be a drop in morale and willingness to participate.

The best remedy for fatigue is the right resources from the start. This includes not only your standard timeframe and financial resources but also the best human resources. It's often a pointless endeavor to task a group with say, finding a new product design solution, but then not having the best quality experts on the team or consultants to help ensure that the sustainability criteria can be met.

Fatigue can also be brought about through a lack of hope as a result of constant exposure to negative concepts about the future. There is no shortage of media coverage on the extreme weather events and catastrophic predictions of climate change. Since this adds up to 'topic fatigue', people naturally start to feel anxiety and stress as a result of the negative framing (Schumann, 2018).

GETTING PAST THE 3 F'S

The three F's play out in different ways, but nearly every organization will have a combination of them that affects their progress toward full-systems transformation.

Consider how you are framing the challenges: are you using positive messaging to get people motivated? What language are you using, and could this be evoking frames or biases that are counter-productive to your change goals?

Everyone responds differently to fear, so work to identify how your teams can be supported to override any natural fear responses.

Reflect on your own reactions and responses to messaging and communication about big issues like climate change. By learning from ourselves, we can often become better leaders and support those around us to overcome their own limiting forces.

There is no exact formula to busting through biases. Context and people, culture and conventions all play into the mix. Thus, you will need to develop your own unique approach to overriding these issues.

Checking in with your team about any anxieties they have will open up a dialogue for a more constructive conversation about the reality of the crises we face.

Additionally, pre-planning to avoid burn-out for teams working to tackle these big complex problems will ensure that they maintain motivation and creativity.

HOW LIMITING FORCES IMPACT YOU

REFLECT

Think about the recent exposures you have had to big global issues (such as climate change, Covid, talent retention, etc.) and consider how you reacted to the information.

Is there an issue that you're feeling fatigued around? How about one that seems easiest to avoid? After you have identified these, consider what alternative approaches you could employ to rewrite the script and take action in a positive way.

GOAL

Use reflexive thinking (learning from experiences you've had) to see how framing, fear and fatigue are applicable in your current worldview and then take action to overcome this.

1-HOUR WORKSHOP IDEA

Explore the impacts of a global issue like climate change for 20 minutes; then spend 20 minutes in pairs discussing how this made them feel and if they've discovered any personal avoidance tactics.

To finish, spend 20 minutes developing a list of actions and opportunities that are tangible, practical ways that your company and the individuals in it can take action to overcome the issue. This will also help to alleviate the fear and avoidance that may have been discussed earlier in the workshop.

☐ DATE COMPLETED _______________________

ADDITIONAL BARRIERS TO CULTURAL CHANGE

1. Pre-Existing Power Structures
Invested in maintaining the status quo, the dinosaur mindset of avoiding pressing issues like climate change, or those that have more to lose by taking action than perpetuating inaction.

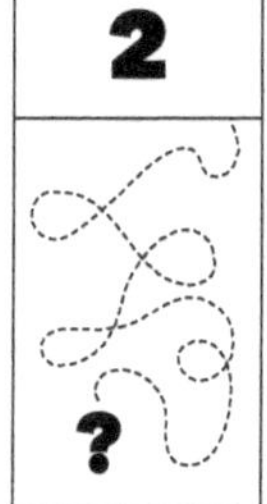
2. Fear, or Failure of the Unknown
Manifests itself as being part of a change process that is seen as too progressive or doesn't fit the current worldview that the person has.

3. Personality Types
We are all different, and some people have flexible mindsets while some are fixed. Some people love challenges, while others need to see a process before they commit to being involved.

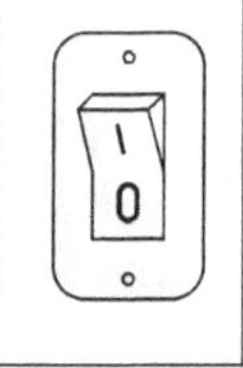
4. Perceived Loss of Power
Power is a resource that we often cling to once we get it. The perception that this power will be lost as a result of the change leads many people to maintain their current position.

5. Myths and Rumors
Stories about past changes can evoke fear or resentment within organizations that tend to have many folklores shared among teams.

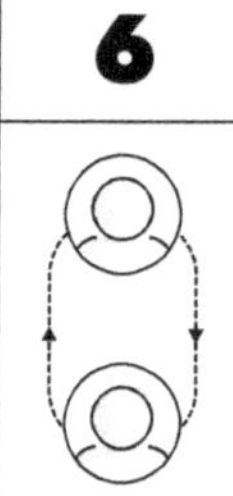
6. No or Low Consultation
Often leads to people feeling excluded or imposed on by the change; by co-designing the process, you can ensure that there is buy-in right from the start and through the process.

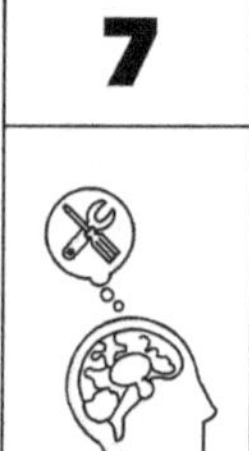
7. Personal Impact of Change
Whether it will require someone to learn a new skill or be given more work, they may perceive it as unfair. Without seeing immediate benefits, it can create resistance and resentment, limiting the process.

8. Lack of Training
The right pace and level of training are needed to equip people with the skills and support they need to adopt the new changes. For example, sustainability skills training.

9. Habit Comfort
We are habitual beings who often find it hard to break free of established routines, unless we are already going through a life disruption or if there is a feasible motivation to create a new habit.

10. Preconceived Ideas
What the change will result in, which is particularly problematic when it comes to addressing climate change, as people often have their own frames that can potentially be limiting.

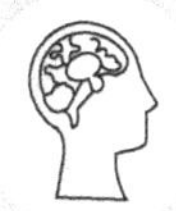

EXPLORING THE FORCES THAT LIMIT CHANGE

REFLECT

Identify the forces and barriers that affect your organization's willingness to adopt change. Does one have a greater force than another and if so, why do you think that is?

GOAL

By considering exploring the limiting forces affecting your company culture, you can design ways to overcome these right from the start.

1-HOUR WORKSHOP IDEA

Using this worksheet, complete a force field analysis with your team.

FORCE FIELD ANALYSIS

Adapted from Kurt Lewin, 1946

Add up the numbers to see the strength of each force. You may find forces FOR change that are weak and need bolstering, or conversely forces AGAINST change that are too strong to intervene in at this time.

LEFT SIDE: Write in all the forces that could motivate the change to happen (they can be positive or negative).

RIGHT SIDE: Write in all the forces that are working against the change happening.

Number each force from 1 to 5:
1 = weak influence
5 = strong influence

FORCES FOR CHANGE

FORCES AGAINST CHANGE

THE STATUS QUO

☐ DATE COMPLETED ______________________________

2.4 ACTIVATING ORGANIZATIONAL CHANGE

All management teams getting started or expanding a sustainability initiative should understand and know how to enact effective organizational change in ways that don't foster or fuel resentment or inertia.

Any change is fundamentally about altering the status quo, which is bound to affect the pre-established equilibrium and thus bring about a short period of instability. This is why change initiatives are often met with resistance.

The key to success in organizational change is a mix of:

- Open dialogue (to reframe the challenges as opportunities)
- Collaboration (ensuring processes are co-created)
- Motivation (designing incentive structures to create conditions for creativity).

People want to feel like they have agency in the process and that any grievances are heard and respected.

BRIGHT SPOTS: Likewise, you should celebrate small wins and highlight the bright spots of success to establish the new normal, but be mindful of over-celebrating insignificance, as this can create a sense of premature accomplishment restricting further action.

CO-CREATION: A way of inviting a process of change with your key stakeholders, rather than dictating it. Consider how you can invite different groups to be involved in the development and delivery of your change initiative. Ensure that everyone has a voice and opportunity to express their fears or concerns so that these can be addressed rather than dismissed.

Co-creation is about working through the uncomfortable aspects of not knowing how the future will be and being willing to have diversity of thoughts in the innovation process.

If you are going to opt for a big ambitious change all at once, make sure that you have implementation stages in place to ensure that the big goal is achievable. Many companies get caught making big claims, like achieving '100% carbon neutral by 2030', going fully recyclable, etc. and forget that they need a way to achieve that goal by starting right away. They will also need a team with the technical skills to deliver on the goals and get full buy-in from the entire company.

Designed and delivered in an inviting and considerate way, many people welcome well-planned and timely change initiatives, especially if there is a pent-up demand for it — which when it comes to values, climate actions and social equity, there is a significant demand from workers through to customers.

BUSINESS ETHICS

Much of the motivation around integrating sustainability into business operations and the workplace at large is due to the ethical implications of not doing so. Increasingly we are seeing a global push toward social and environmental responsibility, with more and more workers, customers and clients demanding that corporate culture adopt an ethical and moral framework relevant to today. As such, when it comes to taking action, you'll need to combine ethics, leadership and trust.

Like all ethical frameworks that govern society, business ethics change over time based on the values and moral codes of the day.

In business the need for good, transparent, fair and morally appropriate legal structures, operations and governance is critical for the long term viability of the organization. Things like corruption, insider trading, bribery, discrimination, workplace cultures, financial misconduct or any form of illegal or immoral conduct will all tear a company apart, either through the exposure of these practices or through the legal proceedings that may result from illegitimate behaviors.

TRANSPARENCY: A core part of sustainability, it's about companies being open about what they are doing and allowing other parties to review and confirm that sustainable actions are being taken.

ETHICS: A set of moral codes that govern the behaviors of individuals within a society or system. Many factors play into the conditions that influence this, but certainly culture and ideological underpinnings affect this in great ways. Leadership is also fundamental for setting the tone of what's right and wrong, so ethics starts from the top.

CODE OF ETHICS

A Code of Ethics shares the guiding principles that support decision making and sets out the moral code of conduct for individuals within the organization.

It is designed to support honesty and integrity while ensuring that the mission and values of the business/organization are aligned with the conduct of its staff and stakeholders.
Certain professionals, like doctors, have their own codes of ethical conduct that govern the actions and set standard values for all who are a part of it. Many people also have their own personal code of conduct that helps them make ethical decisions when faced with complexity of decision making.

Creating a company-wide Code of Ethical Conduct that connects with your wider social and environmental values and goals will help to align your team and set the tone for the organization as a whole.

CORPORATE GOVERNANCE AND LEADERSHIP

Managers and organizational leaders may find ethics a daunting and perhaps even confusing topic to address within their organization. If your company has mainly operated without an ethical code of conduct or consideration of the impacts of your actions outside of financial reporting, then no wonder, as this would be entirely new!

To make things more complex, everyone has different values based on their own life experiences, ideologies and political perspectives. However, the need for leadership to set the tone and standards is so critical in the success of a business, and ethical codes should be designed as bipartisan, bias-avoiding frameworks that clearly communicate the

TYPES OF THINGS AN ETHICAL CODE OF CONDUCT SHOULD INCLUDE

- Human Rights policies

- Environmental policies

- Privacy policies and approaches

- Hiring and diversity policies

- Leadership and governance

- Workers' rights and supply chain ethics

- Supplier engagement policies

- Commitment to excellence

- Care and considerations

- Respect and integrity

- Legal process and adherence

- Social media and communication

- Marketing practices

- Product safety

- Conflict management and resolution

- International activities including dealings with regimes

- Adherence to certain legislation, such as international declarations

- Rights and obligations

- Anti-racism and bias

CREATING A CODE OF CONDUCT

REFLECT

Using the template below, write your own personal code of conduct.

GOAL

Think about your personal values and plan for how you'd like to react when facing complex decisions.

1-HOUR WORKSHOP IDEA

If you already have an organizational code of conduct, assess it as a team and see where and how you may consider improving it. If you don't already, then create your first draft together!

CODE OF CONDUCT	Consider all aspects of your current and desired actions and how you can close the gap between the two; then summarize it in one statement.

MY PROFESSIONAL ACTIONS	**MY LIFESYTLE CHOICES**	**MY PERSONAL RELATIONSHIPS**	**MY COMMUNITY CONTRIBUTIONS**
CURRENT	CURRENT	CURRENT	CURRENT
DESIRED	DESIRED	DESIRED	DESIRED

MY PERSONAL CODE OF CONDUCT IN ONE SUMMARY STATEMENT

☐ DATE COMPLETED _______________________________

importance of doing business in ways that don't harm people, the planet or misdirect its customers.

There are many things that leaders need to consider when it comes to setting up ethical conduct, and of course it's riddled with complexities that may be time consuming to navigate. But it's also essential for good business, company morale and general guidance on how to do good whilst doing good business.

Integrity-based management is on the rise, and without a Code of Ethics and a clear moral stance on important issues like climate change, leaders risk falling behind.

TRUST AND TRANSPARENCY

Most companies sell products and services to customers who have to trust that they will be providing the best quality for the money that they are willing to pay. If trust is lost, then oftentimes, so are the customers.

Making false or misleading claims about safety, performance or sustainability quickly leads to a decay of trust between customers and corporations. The use of socialwashing and greenwashing erode trust, misdirect customers and set progress back. When companies are caught making claims that they can't back up with science and data, or they attempt to misdirect or mislead customers, they are green or social washing. This affects reputation and reduces morale within the company, so there are many net gains from taking steps to ensure that this does not happen.

This type of trust erosion also applies to lobbying and front groups that invest in or set up organizations that help misdirect the understanding or opinion of a company's actions — such as when a company has a run of bad press and they hire a company to communicate the outcomes in a different light. This spin doctoring of the facts often comes back to bite the company later, through exposés or even legal proceedings.

The key thing is that when an organization takes action, communicates something or even does something wrong, the way it is handled will depend on the ethics of the leaders and the moral codes of

"Traceability is the ability to identify and trace the history, distribution, location and application of products, parts and materials, to ensure the reliability of sustainability claims, in the areas of human rights, labour (including health and safety), the environment and anti-corruption."

- UN Global Compact

the organization as a whole. This then will affect the trust, or lack thereof, that stakeholders have in the organization.

That's why transparency is so important, especially in the entire supply chain. Being open and honest about the process, outcomes and yes, even mistakes, generates more trust.

VISIBILITY: Being able to accurately identify and collect data from all the links in your supply chain. Disclosure is about communicating information internally and externally and avoiding being opaque in any of your supply chain areas.

2.5 TOOLS FOR ENABLING CHANGE

THE ENABLING CHANGE CURVE

The Change Curve is a tool used by many sectors wanting to embrace a change journey; there are several variations that you can find online, which are all adapted from psychiatrist Elisabeth Kubler-Ross's work on personal transition in grief and bereavement. It helps to frame the stages that people may experience when confronted with the realization that change is happening, and needed.

From the initial shock, we tend to progress through declining stages of denial, anger, bargaining and then depression. From the pits of despair, we can start to progress our way out of the negative emotions and limiting forces to then accept the change, take actions, embrace the new state and open up future possibilities.

ENABLING CHANGE CURVE

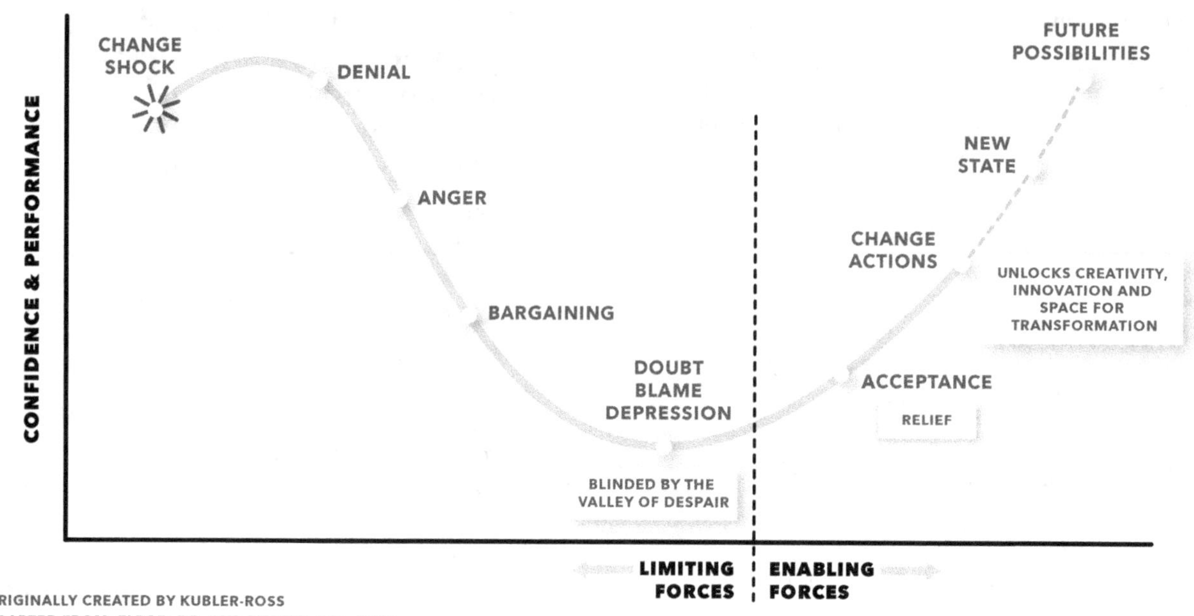

The original change curve ends at "change actions" (see diagram on previous page), but we've adapted this to create the Enabling Change Curve, adding on the upward progress that can occur after acceptance. This shows the possibility for expanding innovation and a positive future through acknowledging limiting forces and then progressing to enabling ones.

A well-designed change intervention can take a different journey, one that hopefully bypasses the pit of despair stage! This is all about how you design the change journey.

Looking at the Enabling Change Curve, can you think of how your own journey has been with any big change? What about your experience with the Covid pandemic?

Some organizations get stuck in the valley of despair, not quite able to look forward and see the potential of the bright future that awaits them if they start to accept that change is needed and understand that they can evolve through the challenges to a new future, one that is driven by sustainability, equity and greater value creation.

Sustainability is by far one of the biggest challenges of our time, and all challenges are opportunities in disguise — it just takes foresight, innovation and a willingness to move through these stages to get to a better outcome. Try using the Enabling Change Curve to map your process of transformation.

THEORY OF CHANGE TOOL

Another great tool to use in enacting change is the Theory of Change (TOC) tool. This is a stepped approach to setting impact goals that define the actions needed to get desired outcomes that will lead to your change goal.

It's a description or illustration of your approach, be it at a project level or organizational one. By creating a clear roadmap, you outline what is

A Theory of Change is a framework that helps outline a hypothesis and pathway for taking action to make change happen.

needed to achieve set goals that follows a flow of steps which helps people see, "If we do X, then Y will happen."

At an organization-wide level, the processes allow for an in-depth exploration of the values, mission, beliefs and worldview that drive the organization forward.

It serves as a definition of your change philosophy that should filter through all of the work you do, be understood by all employees and stakeholders and provide a roadmap for success. The process of creating a TOC at this level should also reflect on stakeholders, internal organizational structures, processes and the capacity to ensure that the TOC

and the organization's operations align.
A Theory of Change is created by mapping backwards from the desired outcomes through to the actions needed to be taken in order to get there.

For example, you want to change the way people view sustainability within your organization, so you start by setting that as a clear objective and then move back through the different stages. The outputs are the tangible things that show how people's perceptions change. Actions need to be taken to get to the outputs, and all actions you take will require resources and inputs to make them happen. This provides a clear map of what you need to do to get to the outcome that you want.

THEORY OF CHANGE

PROBLEM

IF WE DO THIS....

INPUTS

WHAT WE INVEST & RESOURCES NEEDED TO TAKE THE ACTIONS

ACTIONS

WHAT ACTIONS WE NEED TO TAKE TO ACHIEVE OUTPUTS

THEN WE EXPECT THESE...

OUTPUTS

WHAT GOODS AND SERVICES ARE PRODUCED
WHAT WE NEED TO SEE TO KNOW THE IMPACT WAS MADE

OUTCOMES

SHORT AND LONG TERM RESULTS OF OUR ACTIONS

IMPACT

THERE ARE FIVE MAIN ASPECTS:

1. Defining the problems and setting the impact goal

2. Defining the outcomes that will achieve your impact goal

3. Setting what outputs you will need to see that will lead to the outcomes

4. Listing the actions you need to take to get the outputs

5. Listing the resources and inputs that you need to do the actions

MASTERING CHANGE

Change is constant and goes through many ebbs and flows. When dealing with change, it's important to be in tune with the process, be aware of the dynamics at play and find ways to participate within them.

Any new skill requires curiosity and tenacity to get to a level of mastery.

HERE ARE SOME TIPS FOR MASTERING CHANGE:

- Accept that everything is constantly changing all the time, so whatever you do is an intervention into the system around you and has the potential to offer dynamic change.

- Seek out the relationships that make up the status quo of the system.

- Always account for delays.

- Have contingency plans.

- Measure, but also know that there are biases in measurements, so observe the unobvious.

- Be okay with chaos; find ways to enjoy the dynamics it brings.

- Learn to love the problems you are faced with and find delight in what dealing with them can offer.

- Avoid laying blame; instead, find connections.

- Remember there is no failure, just opportunities to uncover new things.

On that last point, it is inevitable that you will encounter challenges and setbacks in designing any form of change. Challenges are actually a great learning opportunity (once you get over the stress and pain they may cause), so when you encounter one, try to develop a data log inside your mind to help build your resilience bank and personal capacity to design around the issue the next time.

In systems thinking, there is this great concept that the easy way out often leads back in. So, discovering how to learn from adversity and challenges is a critical part of the capacity-building mindset of any effective organizational change-maker.

Problems often hold their own solution. It's your quest to figure out what that is, and how you, as one individual in a bigger system within your unique sphere of influence, can activate your own agency to find the sweet spots for leveraging positive change.

There are no quick fixes to complex problems, and nearly all of the issues we encounter are indeed complex. Thus, change does take time.

Overcoming reductive and linear thought processes, uncovering biases and cognitive dissonance, being willing to learn through failure and building a robust, curious, systems-loving mindset are all important tools for effecting change that are all available to you.

We all have the capacity to have a positive influence on the world around us. So, let's dive into the practical tools for enacting a systems-level transformation to sustainability.

REFLECTION ACTIVITY

ORGANIZATIONAL THEORY OF CHANGE

REFLECT

Do you already have a Theory of Change at your organization? If so, read it and think about what you may change to include full-systems sustainability. If not, search for an example in your industry to get a feel for what a Theory of Change looks like.

GOAL

Define what it is that your organization is doing in order to bring about, facilitate, foster or enhance change.

1-HOUR WORKSHOP IDEA

Using the template below, as a team, create or revise your organization's Theory of Change.

THEORY OF CHANGE | Consider all aspects of your current and desired actions and how you can close the gap between the two; then summarize it in one statement.

◀············· **START HERE AND WORK BACKWARDS**

PROBLEM	**INPUTS**	**ACTIONS**	**OUTPUTS**	**OUTCOMES**
Current situation & desired vision?	*What resources & investements are needed to take the actions?*	*What actions do we need to take to achieve the outputs?*	*What results do we need to see happen to know we made an impact?*	*Immediate and long term results of the actions?*

☐ DATE COMPLETED ________________________

RECOMMENDATIONS FOR IMPLEMENTING AN ORGANIZATIONAL THEORY OF CHANGE

- Clarity is key! Keep it short and simple, get right to the point and show the connections between your goals along with the ways you will achieve them.

- Create through participation. A good TOC is developed collaboratively through key teams and stakeholders and usually has several rounds of iteration. Seek out different perspectives so that your final outcome is clear and achievable.

- Be realistic about your resources (inputs) and aspirational with your goals.

- Use the TOC to inform policy and procedures so that there is alignment.

- Give it time. Allow enough time to develop and reflect on the outcome so you get to something that has longevity.

- Build on what you have already done. Reflect and synthesize on past projects and approaches to see what has or has not worked.

  Use this as part of the development process to get to the essence of what you want to achieve in the future through the experiences you have had in the recent past.

- Reference. If you are using data or making assumptions, be sure to reference them so it's obvious how numbers have been developed and then can be adjusted when things change.

- Don't forget who you are seeking to serve. Most organizations are about making an impact in some way, so be clear on who you are seeking to support in your work. Ensure that they are involved in the process and that the change approaches are welcomed by them.

- Be willing to change yourself. Sometimes doing this process will bring to light areas that you need to change, so be willing to adapt and adjust where necessary.

- See it is a living thing. You will certainly learn new things as you enact your TOC, so you should periodically reflect and adjust where needed.

  Set a review time (say in 2 or 5 years) when you release it as a reminder to do so. It may stay the same, but reassessing it will help define your goals and check in with your methods of achieving them.

PRACTICAL TIPS FOR ACTIVATING CHANGE

- Host an off-site or all-hands meeting to define the shared goals and vision for the change. Introduce benchmarking and doing case studies to anchor your team in the right mindset so that they see the reasons why change is not only needed, but also beneficial.

- Create a diverse working group and set very clear goals that have many small wins to keep the team focused and motivated.

- Increase buy-in by asking for feedback and inputs on things like policy development or cultural changes as they are being created.

- Make it exciting by running a hackathon or ideation session to solicit ideas from team members.

- Develop an effective and engaging internal communications strategy that is updated based on progress.

- Test to ensure messaging or change approach design is triggering the desired response in your community/team. Be willing to change your method or direction if the initial approach is not working as planned.

- Make it fun! Offer rewards or gamify the experience through challenges (we dive into this on page 128 of Part 3).

- Provide training and a support structure to staff.

- Don't drag the process on too long or be wishy-washy about what you are doing.

- Unite people around a common goal.

- Measure and share progress.

- Get high-level buy-ins, such as the CEO or the board; have them make clear statements and be present to motivate staff.

- Find a change model that will work for your organization.

- If you are hiring new staff to manage the change, ensure that they are aligned to your values and have the experience needed to overcome barriers.

- Identify and address any cultural issues or internal grievances efficiently and respectfully.

- Pilot, experiment and adapt — all change journeys require some adjustments to the process to make it work!

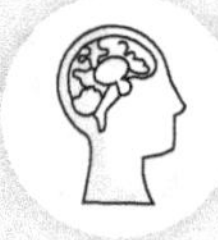

REFLECTION ACTIVITY

PART 2 RECAP

(1) How would you define your existing workplace/company culture?

(2) What cultural changes do you need to make to open up the possibility
of full systems transformation?

(3) How do you personally relate to change? Do you believe it to be hard? Does it excite
you? Is it a mixture of both? What do you need to do in order to find an opportunity in
embracing this type of change?

(4) How are the 3 F's (Fear, Fatigue, Framing) affecting your business? What are three
strategies that you can implement to help overcome these barriers?

(5) Reflecting on the Ethical Code of Conduct that you completed, what needs to happen
next for your organization to leverage it in order to advance sustainability? If your
organization has not yet created a Code of Conduct, what are the next steps that you
can take to design and implement one?

(6) How can you use the Theory of Change tool to advance your change initiatives
within your organization?

(7) What does individual agency look like in your organization? How can leadership
(Management, CEO, C Suite) both set the tone for activating company-wide change
and better support individual agency for every worker, no matter their role?

(8) Reflecting on the aspects of Mastering Change laid out on page 88, which three tips
do you feel are the highest priority for your organization to consider?v

☐ DATE COMPLETED ________________________

PART 3

THE SUSTAINABILITY IN BUSINESS 3D FRAMEWORK

I recently stayed at a major hotel chain in Brussels for an event. I was impressed by the sustainability initiatives they had integrated into their customer experience, done so well that even fellow guests were talking about how much more they enjoyed the experience.

Instead of offering single-use plastic water bottles in the rooms, they had a water station that offered cold, hot and seltzer water on every floor. Designed in a very engaging and beautiful way, the reusable water bottles provided in each room made it enjoyable to venture out to refill them from the station.

I also noticed after my room had been cleaned that they'd used bicarbonate of soda + vinegar, a long known hygienic and sustainable cleaning solution, with a touch of peppermint or eucalyptus oil to leave a beautiful fragrance in the room.

There was no sign that asked me to reuse my towels, just hooks to hang them on, and no removal of them in-between cleans. I have always found those little signs so commonly placed in hotel bathrooms — you know, the ones that ask you to save the planet by reusing your towel — to be a classic case of greenwashing. Whilst reducing laundry will have a small impact reduction, without many other actions being taken such as eliminating single-use products and offering low-carbon food options, the towel reuse does not equal a good sustainability outcome.

It's also been shown by studies that the messaging on these signs will determine how people act (Gössling, et al, 2019).For example, if one sign says "62% of people who stay in this room reuse their towel", the number of people who then do that increased by 6.8% in comparison to signs that ask people to "do the right thing" and reuse their towel. This is because humans follow social cues and are happy to go along with what everyone else is doing. This is called following normative cues.

So, by intentionally designing experiences like beautiful water refill stations or clear communication of the desired behaviours in given scenarios, we can create new types of norms that result in beneficial outcomes.

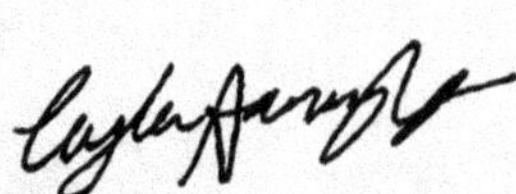

3.1 THE SUSTAINABILITY IN BUSINESS 3D FRAMEWORK

Every action taken has an impact, and many of the social and environmental issues that we are seeking to design out of the system through sustainability are locked in through everyday decisions made in business. Thus, in this section, we'll first dive into the best-practice methods used to assess your business's impacts, and then we'll define techniques used for designing policies to change them toward full systems sustainability.

To make the process of impact assessment more accessible, we created the Sustainability in Business 3D Framework. Based on the operational, product and experiential impacts that all businesses have, there are 18 important areas of impact, as shown in the diagram below.

OPERATIONS: The energy, water, waste, infrastructure, travel and procurement that the company consumes and produces in order to do business.

PRODUCTS: Everything that is produced by a company as part of their offering into the economy. These have significant supply chain, material, natural resource and waste impacts and should be considered in relation to full life product stewardship across the manufacturing, materials, packaging, retail, consumer use and end of life.

THE 3D FRAMEWORK IMPACT AREAS

 The culture fostered and services created by an organization for customers and employees. This involves looking at the direction, space, cognitive experience, communication, engagement and journey created as part of your business offerings.

Combined this three-stage framework is designed to help you take action to ensure your organization is continually improving and evolving how you run your operations, design your products and engage with your customers and stakeholders so that sustainability becomes an integral part of your organization's DNA.

Whilst there are many areas your business will need to assess and transform, not all of the 18 areas will be of major impact. Additionally, there will be industry-specific areas to consider. For example, a tech company has a different set of impacts to a hotel or a packaged food company.

It's likely, however, that no matter what size your company is, you will need to assess your operational impacts of energy, waste, water, infrastructure, procurement and travel, as these are often the foundations of a company's day-to-day environmental impacts.

Likewise, since you're producing and buying products and/or services that rely on complex supply chains, you'll need to look at the materials used, the design approaches, the end-of-life impacts and the opportunities to redesign the delivery of your products and services to the market in sustainable and circular ways.

Finally, you'll want to consider your stakeholders' experience. From your employees to your customers and the ways that they engage with your organization, the more you consider all of the touchpoints associated with the experience offering and how you direct customers to interact more sustainably with your company and its products/services, the higher successes you will have when transforming to a sustainable business. Afterall, their actions add up to your impacts.

Here's an example — say you're in the hotel business. You sell the service of rooms and accommodation, which both have clear operational impacts by way of the cleaning products used, consumables offered, energy and water used, restaurant catering, etc. You can assess these impacts and work to make improvements through purchasing renewable energy, growing food on site, composting food waste, and using green cleaning products. But you can also provide direction to customers to ensure that their behaviors during their stay are more sustainable — such as refillable water bottles and beautiful water stations instead of disposable bottles (like at my hotel in Brussels), discounted green transportation options and clearly-communicated goals on your collective performance. When you see it as a collaboration between your company and your customers, you start to change the relationship by design.

To get started, establish the major priority areas that immediately affect your business and indicate a level of importance for each of these areas. Use the activity worksheet on the next page to prioritize where you will start your impact assessment journey.

ENVIRONMENTAL AUDITING

Auditing is part of any good sustainability approach. It's a process of considering the direct and indirect impacts of your company's actions by understanding and working with the entire value chain and taking full responsibility for the social and environmental impacts of the business activities.

Auditing offers a systemic scrutiny of your activities to develop a more detailed perspective on what you are actually doing, thereby uncovering the impacts of your actions and thus, the opportunities for transforming them.

Environmental auditing is about measuring, comparing and reflecting before actioning change. Then, you measure again to ensure that you have obtained positive results. Audits create a benchmark for future assessment and improvements.

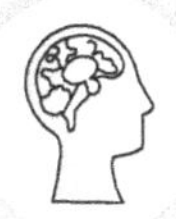

FAMILIARIZE YOURSELF WITH THE 3D SUSTAINABILITY IN BUSINESS FRAMEWORK

REFLECT

Before diving into the framework (review in more detail on page 111), use this worksheet to consider your best assessment for which areas your organization has the most impacts, and set priorities.

GOAL

Begin familiarizing the areas of impact in direct context with your organization and prime your brain to do deeper assessments for the highest impact areas.

1-HOUR WORKSHOP IDEA

After completing the worksheet, have a team discussion about your company's main priorities for taking action. Set targets for immediate, mid and long-term goals to address those top priorities.

PRIORITY LEVELS | Assign each of the 6 subcategories a level of priority for your industry or company to address from highest priority (1) to least (6).

OPERATIONAL	PRODUCT	EXPERIENTIAL
_____ ENERGY	_____ CUSTOMER USE	_____ COGNITION
_____ PROCUREMENT	_____ RETAIL	_____ JOURNEY
_____ WASTE	_____ END OF LIFE	_____ ENGAGEMENT
_____ TRAVEL	_____ SUPPLY CHAINS	_____ COMMUNICATION
_____ WATER	_____ MATERIALS	_____ SPACE
_____ INFRASTRUCTURE	_____ PACKAGING	_____ DIRECTION

☐ DATE COMPLETED ________________________

This is why the 3D framework covers the operational, product and experiential impacts, instead of just one area. Impacts occur across all aspects of an organization's activities in the economy, and auditing is one of the main ways you will gain a clear understanding and a data set to benchmark against.

One thing to avoid is using an audit process to control versus explore. Auditing should be about uncovering aspects of your systems that were not obvious at first so that the data and insights can be used as the foundations for creating better outcomes. This is not a race to the bottom or a tick-the-box activity (although checklists can be very helpful in ensuring that the right data is collected regularly).

ENVIRONMENTAL AUDIT OBJECTIVES

- Determine & document current status

- Understand & improve environmental performance

- Improve management processes

- Increase awareness of impacts

- Develop and employ environmental management systems

- Reduce risks & liabilities

- Develop benchmarks

- Promote sustainability within your organization

- Account for environmental consequences, both foreseen and unforeseen

- Influence future management practices

- Create data that helps fuel organizational change

- Reduce negative impacts from operations

- Measure against your goals

AUDIT PROCESS

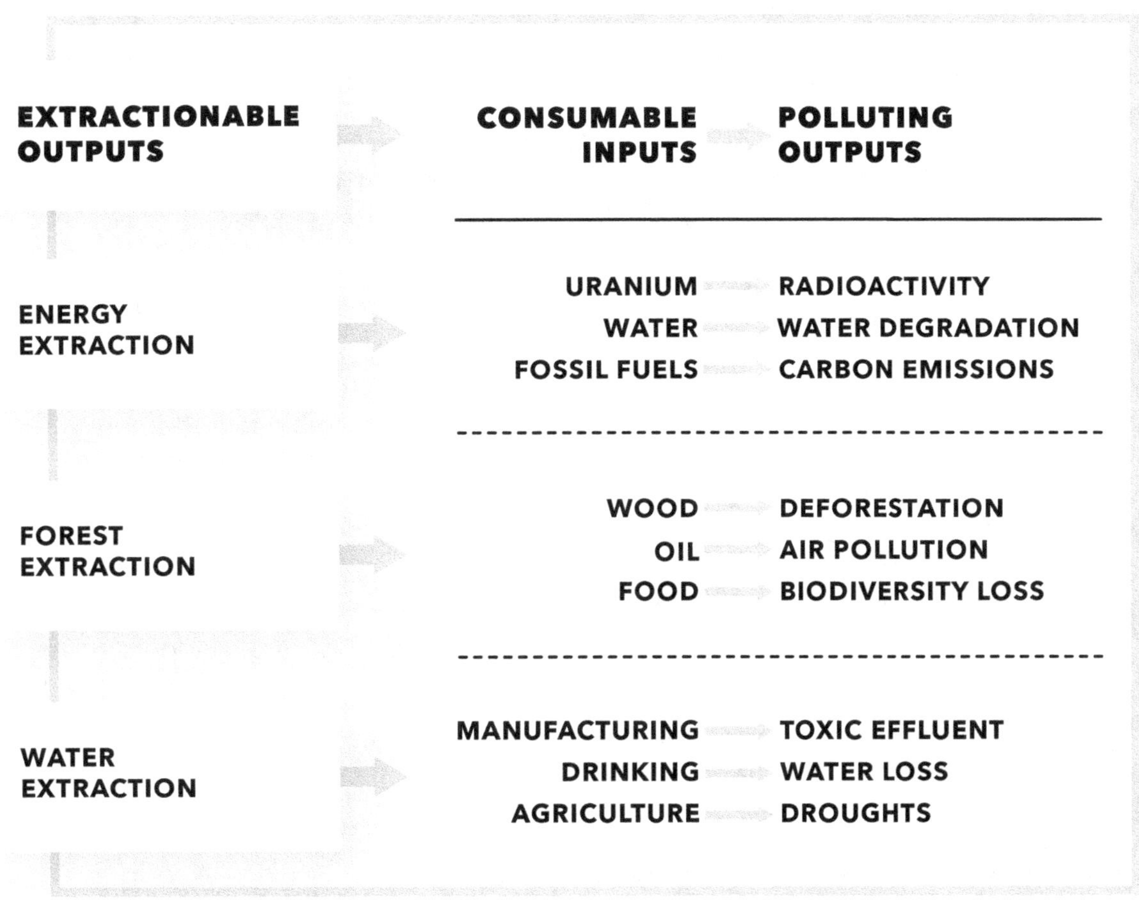

In some industries, certain environmental management regulations are required to be adhered to, but moving beyond compliance should be the goal of all sustainability-focused businesses.

We will get into this in more detail, but the type of audits you may do are waste, energy, procurement, travel, supply chains, water, etc.

ENVIRONMENTAL IMPACT ASSESSMENTS

Every single action has impacts back on the environment in some way; impact assessments help to determine what will happen once an action has been taken.

All operations, along with materials and manufacturing, require inputs. These are resources like raw materials, energy and water which must be first extracted and then fed into the system. As a result, outputs are generated.

Outputs tend to be the cause of an action, such as CO2 from energy use or waste from manufacturing. In environmental impact assessments, you are measuring the effects of inputs and outputs that occur as part of your operations and actions.

By doing this, you gain valuable insights into the resource inputs and pollution outputs of your company. Then you can manage and mitigate them by changing suppliers, processes, designs and policies.

Once you have assessed your impacts, you can then start to develop approaches to transform them through environmental management policies, sustainability strategies or whatever approaches make the most sense for your company.

To clarify, audits and assessments are both tools for identifying and documenting impacts that occur as a result of business decisions and actions. They share some terminology but are utilized in different ways.

An assessment anticipates impacts. It's most commonly conducted before an action is taken in order to explore potential impacts that may occur, whereas an audit is often carried out on something that already exists, such as business operations or supply chains.

Assessments provide information and insights to decision makers on potential impacts so that they can be designed out of the product/business/service; the data that helps inform this is often from an audit. So, they work hand-in-hand to provide insights that can lead to better actions.

Let's look at a couple of examples of how you can use audits and assessments to inform how you manage your impacts.

You will have climate change impacts across several areas of your business, including the energy that powers operations, like an office or worksite, the types of servers hosting your website and the processes used to get your product to market.

By auditing your energy bills, procurement practices, and the products in use, you can assess what your total energy impact is and calculate how this translates as a climate impact (there are many calculators online that help do this). You can then use this data to set your climate reduction targets and change practices within your company.

Another big impact area is waste production. You likely generate solid waste from your office, including general paper, packaging, coffee, food waste, etc., which can be separated quite easily for recycling and organic waste collection. These can then be monitored to document amounts of waste production and contamination.

Waste produced from product development across the supply chain is often the bigger issue. Examples include water run-off from fabric dyes, offcuts from material manufacturing, chemicals used in agriculture, etc.

KEY ACTIONS FROM AUDITS & ASSESSMENTS

- Gain data that will inform your decisions

- Set tangible targets and timeframes for achievement

- Create policies

- Train staff

- Align your stakeholders

- From here, you will see immediate improvements.

You will only be able to reduce these impacts by auditing and mapping your entire supply chain along with all the materials and processes that occur throughout it (jump ahead to page 119 to get started on this).

Sustainable practices around waste can leverage principles of the circular economy, which eliminates waste from the system.

This requires you to find new ways of designing your processes to stop waste or to cycle it back through a well-designed system, which often involves bringing products back into your manufacturing system through reverse supply chain logistics and customer return incentives.

IMPACT ASSESSMENT STANDARDS

Traditionally, environmental impact assessments are done in accordance with local laws, and there are several International Standard Organization (ISO) standards that cover the environmental impact assessment process, output and communication.

There are actually over 300,000 ISO certifications in the ISO 14001 series, currently present in 171 countries around the world (see: www.iso.org).

Some of the important ISO Standards include:

- Environmental management systems

- Environmental auditing and related environmental investigations

- Environmental labeling

- Environmental performance evaluation

- Life cycle assessment

- Greenhouse gas and climate change management + related activities

- Ecolabeling

JUMP TO PAGE 124 FOR A MORE DETAILED LOOK AT ECOLABELING

In the context of the 3D framework, impact assessments are done across all your main business activities to gain clear insights into the way your actions are having impacts from a holistic perspective, rather than an isolated one.

SOCIAL IMPACT ASSESSMENTS

So far we have been focusing on the environmental impact side of things, but there are many social impacts resulting from your operations and activities that need to be assessed and improved.

Social impact assessments measure how your business affects people in a community as well as in society as a whole. After a social impact assessment is done, you can implement approaches that reduce negative social impacts and boost programs that improve positive social impacts.

Social impact assessment requires interaction with the workers along your entire supply chain to ensure that no one is being exploited or harmed and that their labor practices are ethical and fair.

You will need to explore the impacts of your actions on the way of life of the people you are impacting, including the culture, community, health and wellbeing of the people along your entire value chain.

This is about preemptively measuring both the intended and unintended consequences of your actions on society, community and individuals.

Over the past few decades, many people have been working on methodologies that incorporate social impact assessment into robust processes like life cycle assessments. But it is a lot harder to measure impacts on humans than it is on the environment, given that measuring social impacts can be quite subjective.

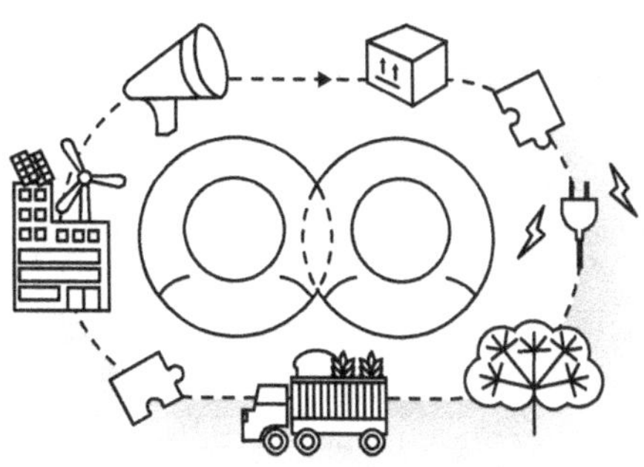

AUDITING AND ASSESSING ENVIRONMENTAL IMPACTS

Start by collecting all the data points that you have access to; this could be your energy/waste/water/travel/purchasing bills or an energy/waste/behavior audit, either done internally or by hiring a specialized agency to collect the data for you. You can broadly do this across the different categories associated with operations and products. There are a few jumping off questions included below to help get you started.

- **OPERATIONAL IMPACTS:** Using data from the last twelve months of your energy/waste/water bills, calculate the current usage and the impacts associated with this. Then identify areas and actions you can take to significantly reduce these. Swap to decarbonized energy sources, implement efficiency measures and change waste providers.

- **RAW MATERIALS:** What is your product made out of (or what resources do your services require to operate), and where does it come from? For example, if you have a plastic component, where do the petrochemicals it's made of originate from? What mines do your metals come from? Which forests do your paper/wood products grow in? How are these materials grown, harvested and processed? Do they have certifications or requirements they need to meet? Are the materials from virgin or recycled sources, and if recycled, how are they collected and processed? What happens to the offcuts and waste products during the material processing?

- **MANUFACTURING:** Where are your products manufactured and/or assembled? How is the factory powered, and under what conditions? What are the steps and ingredients required to create the product at all steps of construction? For example, if you have a product requiring color, what type of dye or ink is used, and how is the waste water handled? If it is in a drought-prone area, are waterless or reduced water practices used? If you have a digital product, where are the servers located, and what environmental considerations are taken for their operating requirements?

- **PACKAGING:** What types of materials are being used in your packaging? Could alternatives be found? Is the packaging optimized for lightweighting and product protection? Are items individually packaged or bulk packaged for transport? Are there clear instructions on the packaging for how to handle it after it's purchased and unboxed?

- **TRANSPORT:** What methods are used to transport your raw materials, packaging and the final goods to the end user? What power sources are used to move them, and what kinds of distances are being crossed? What ports of call are your goods moving though, and what landing policies are in place to ensure compliance on safety testing? Are any tax or safety requirements being bypassed by either using evasion ports or alternative product category codes? Are labels being added in special economic zones or locations with lower tax burdens to take advantage of "made in" manufacturing loopholes?

- **USE:** Are care instructions clear for both maintenance, repair and end of life handling? Are systems set up for clear communication with your customers? Are your environmental policies clearly and transparently communicated and easily accessible? Have you have trained customer service staff to answer sustainability questions? Do your products meet the mandatory labeling requirements for the country they are sold in (not just your HQ country)?

- **END OF LIFE:** Have you optimized your products or services for the circular economy? Have you created a community of users that can support each other through swaps, reuse, recycling, upcycling, etc? Have you created clear and frictionless pathways to re-collect the products you put out into the world? Have you developed methods of either remanufacturing or collaborating with other companies who can use the parts you are unable to reintegrate? Have you checked that the recycling facilities in the location your products are being used are able to reuse or resell the material and are not just storing it or landfilling it?

- **CONSIDER:** The three main areas of life-carrying capacity: air, water and Earth. How are your products at each stage impacting (either negatively or positively) the air quality, water quality and ground health, and therefore the humans not just in the immediate vicinity, but also in the wider globe?

- **DATA:** Once you have data, segregate it across the 5 main categories (raw materials, manufacturing, packaging, transportation, use, end of life) so you can develop baseline information on where your impacts are occurring. If you don't know how to do the data collection and synthesis, consider using a third-party platform or hiring consultants to ensure you get the right data to establish your baseline.

- **REMEMBER:** You are responsible for your own waste production. If you hire a third party, assign someone or a team to work directly with them, and whenever possible, have someone physically visit the sites of raw material through to transportation, run test cases for consumer use and visit end-of-life points.

- What other information can you collect about the impact areas? Use scenarios, behaviors – for example, why is something using a lot of energy to be manufactured or used? What is driving the motivation of your end user to engage with your product or service? These are qualitative aspects of your assessment that can help you gain additional data to influence your understanding of the impact areas. These will differ greatly depending on your end user (gender, country, age, cultural influences, economic context, etc.), so you may need to create several scenarios.

- Different impact categories have different assessment types, such as doing an energy audit or using the Greenhouse Gas Protocol to assess carbon emission against it. There are life cycle assessments and ecological footprints for products, so make sure you have the best assessment approach for each of your impact areas.
- Think beyond carbon offset trades. Instead, you could buy and protect a large area of mangrove, rehabilitate a local ecosystem, divert money away from oil industry investments, support local social and health programs or fund scholarships for underserved communities. Just be sure that one action is not your sole focus and/or used to create a false perception of your social and environmental performance.

- Stay up to date on new policies, regulations and transparency registers in other countries as they develop. Start early so that as these ripple out to more and more parts of the world, you don't have to catch up when they start to affect you.

- There are coalitions in many industries that focus on your specific impact areas; consider joining them for accountability and community resource pooling.

- Reassess regularly to see how you are tracking against your baseline data. It also helps to see what an industry standard is and how you are performing against your peers.

- Be clear and transparent about your progress, what your goals are, what you have accomplished so far and how you benchmark. Report not just on what you aspire to achieve, but also what you have achieved and in what timeline. Consider integrating your sustainability goals into your annual report, along with the costs, benefits, challenges and opportunities you have faced and either overcome or are developing a plan of action around.

CONSIDERATIONS IN SOCIAL IMPACT

- Work with affected communities to understand how actions will result in impacts that affect them and explore possible community-derived ways of addressing these.

- Get proof from your suppliers that all their workers are paid an appropriate rate — not just in line with the going rate in the local community, but a rate that allows them to have a living wage, live comfortably, upskill, provide education for their children, access food and clean water and provide the potential for upward mobility in their community.

- Seek out trusted third-party verification on claims and engage validation services that will perform regular inspections and follow-ups.

- Physically visit the factories, mines or production facilities yourself to confirm the suppliers' claims and ensure that your standards are being upheld.

- If you don't already have a set of standards for working conditions, create one. Then share it with your suppliers, have them commit to it and support them in meeting any costs or time requirements to level up.

- Invest in helping your manufacturing facilities improve where needed, and if possible, form collaborations with other companies who use the same factories to create cohesive and aligned conditions of work.

- Check for subcontractors or suppliers, cottage industry outsourcing or other undisclosed methods of meeting timelines.

- Set realistic delivery timelines to avoid unrealistic expectations that force suppliers to outsource to unvetted facilities.

- Seek out manufacturing facilities that provide support for their employees, such as childcare on location, pay rates that don't require onerous overtime in order to meet the cost of living, basic healthcare coverage, regular break and meal times, transportation to the work site, etc.

- Check the raw materials and Material Safety Data Sheets (MSDS) to ensure that the proper safety measures are being put in place and adhered to. There are service providers that can arrange these checks for you.

- Track and monitor where post-manufacturing waste materials are being sent and how they are processed and transported in order to avoid infiltrating local water tables or creating other impacts on the community.

- Track and monitor where pre-manufacturing raw materials are being sourced from and how they are being processed and transported. Ensure that workers are operating in safe conditions.

- Arrange for or request documentation on building inspections to ensure that the stability of the building is maintained, fire codes are in place, exits are clear, and emergency procedures are shared with the employees.

- Require that injury rates are reported each year, and ensure appropriate actions are taken to reduce incidents. This includes providing appropriate healthcare for accidents, along with sick/disability leave. Injuries should not threaten job security.

- Require that on-site job training is provided to increase skills not only in this position but going forward as well. Consider establishing a scholarship program for employees and their families.

- Maintain an HR department for hiring, firing, disputes, salary negotiations, exit interviews and anonymous reporting of concerns.

- Have facilities post your standards of work clearly in a public place so that the employees know their rights.

- Provide proper ventilation, clean water, appropriate bathroom facilities and adequate locations for meals.

- If you provide a service that is impactful on the employees' mental health, provide resources for counseling and other support services.

- Provide clear and transparent pay structures with equivalent pay for equivalent work, regardless of gender, sexual preference, identity, race, or other factors that have historically had pay imbalances. Require that cost of living inflation wages are provided annually.

- Provide paid maternity and paternity leave, short and long-term disability coverage and basic healthcare benefits.

- Consult the local community and implement appropriate projects and initiatives in collaboration with your facilities for social and environmental programs in the areas that you are working within.

- If you work with physical goods, find out where the rejected products go and redivert them to those who could use them. Or, ensure that they are recycled back into your production process.

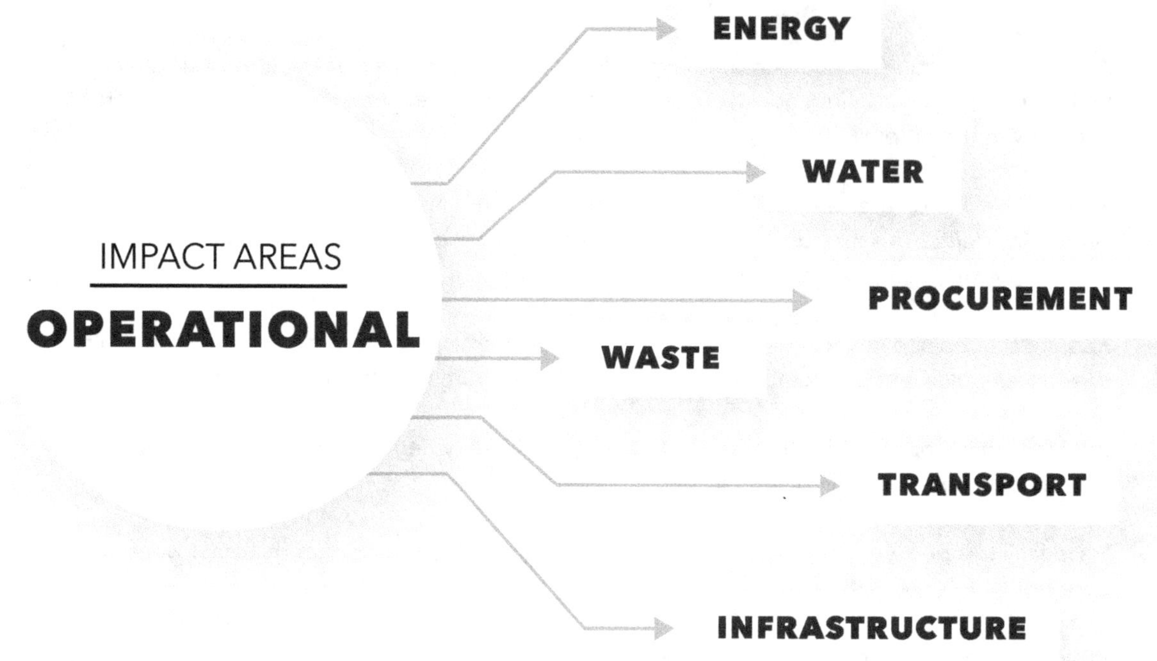

3.2 OPERATIONAL IMPACTS

Operational impacts are those that are created in your daily operations, usually attributed to your offices, warehouses, factories and workforce's activities. Every company has operational impacts; some are obvious and direct, such as energy use, while others are more hidden, such as the impacts associated with products procured to operate the business.

Operational impacts change over time and depend on both your business's actions and your suppliers. There are quick wins like swapping energy sources and purchasing low-carbon catering, as well as long-term strategies that require investment and planning. These include implementing renewable energy systems, providing on-site biodigestion for organic waste and investing in green buildings, for example.

The actions of your service providers will also impact your company's operating impacts. So in order to make improvements and get to a positive operating mode, you should assess your current operations for baseline data to get a full picture of what your current operating impacts are. Then from this, take

action by making decisions and policies to improve. Continue reassessing the data on a regular basis to measure impact improvement as your actions are implemented, and then, set new, more ambitious targets.

Operational impacts are attributed to all the activities that you do inside your office, factory or workspace and that which are required for daily business operations, such as travel and procurement. To make it easy to assess, we have curated six main categories for operational impacts assessment.

ENERGY

Energy use applies to the energy used in your buildings, factories and equipment. The best way to check where you energy and thus carbon impact is at right now is by doing an audit of your past bills, checking energy mix with suppliers, assessing technology impact use on site and via third party suppliers like web servers.

An energy audit also includes monitoring particular sectors of your business/office space to see what is wasting energy over a set period of time (like a week, month, etc.). Are lights turned off, computers powered down and machines operated efficiently? What changes can you make to improve operational efficiency?

Large amounts of energy are used in refrigeration, climate control, lights, technology, machinery and manufacturing processes.

Anything that gets plugged in and thus requires power is worth assessing for its energy use to ensure that it is managed in an energy-efficient way.

ACTIONS TO TAKE:

- Divest from all fossil fuel energy sources. Swap providers or ask for renewable energy.
- Put lights on sensors to have them automatically turn off when not needed.
- Replace high-energy light bulbs with low-energy bulbs.
- Place timers and sleep mode on all energy-using products.
- Use non-centrally controlled heating and cooling so that it can be adjusted by occupants to create the temperature needed.
- Closed refrigeration systems to avoid energy loss.
- Change up work attire to require less heating or cooling in the workplace.
- Maximize natural light and ventilation.
- Use an energy-reading device to check plug-in product energy usage.
- Install alternative energy systems on site, such as solar or wind.
- Design buildings to be passively heated/cooled.
- Provide clear direction to staff and customers on how to operate all electrical products/systems to maximize efficient use.
- Swap to green servers, have good digital hygiene and delete old emails to reduce cloud-based storage.

WATER

Water use applies to the water used in your office buildings, factories, facilities and managed sites. You can benchmark against your water bills to see how much water you are currently using as well as conduct site audits to see where water is being used/wasted.

The main areas of water use for an office or commercial building are in the bathroom and kitchen. How much water the toilet holds and the efficiency of the flush will have big impacts, as will the types of taps, the maintenance of them to reduce leaking and the behaviors of your staff.

Kitchens often use up more water when there are stronger policies around reusables because of the water used in washing; a well-stacked dishwasher is a better option than everyone hand washing their coffee cup.

To get an idea of what your water usage is, view your bills and do a flow test by measuring how many liters of water comes out of your taps for a set period of time (usually 30 seconds). You can do this by timing how long it takes to fill an electric kettle and calculating how much water is coming out of each tap based on how many liters it holds. You can then install flow reducers and sensors to decrease water use.

In factories and production facilities, waste water is a major issue with the water run-off often contributing pollutants to local waterways. Ensure that filtration systems are in place before waste water is released, and reduce the use of toxic materials.

ACTIONS TO TAKE:

- Install flow reduction devices and sensors on tap faucets.
- Have dual-flush toilets with low water usage.
- Create a system for efficient dishwasher stacking and or/washing up procedures.
- In industrial facilities, ensure all wastewater is filtered. Consider biofiltration systems.
- Collect grey water and reuse it in toilets or gardens; consider site-specific ways of redirecting used water from kitchens and hand basins to being reused.
- Install rain water collection tanks on site, and use this for toilet flushing and plant watering.
- In industrial facilities, collect and reuse water where possible.
- On sites ensure that water is managed responsibly and that customers can't leave taps on or waste water.

PROCUREMENT

This encompasses all of your in-house purchases, from office paper, to stationery, desks, technology, raw materials, catering, coffee or whatever else you need to buy to do your business. For an office, the main areas of procurement are stationery, furniture and consumables like coffee, snacks, personal safety and cleaning supplies, toilet paper and any other item you need to do your daily business. If you are a medical facility, then you will have all sorts of other more complex things that you are buying (and disposing of!). What you buy will directly affect your waste production.

Procurement makes up 13-20% of global GDP (World Bank, 2020), so there is massive purchasing power that can be leveraged to create new markets for environmentally-preferable products. Measuring and monitoring what and how frequently you buy products, who they are coming from and what degree of them is wasted will help you develop a sustainable procurement policy.

ACTIONS TO TAKE:

- Check all of your contracts to ensure that you have suppliers who offer green options and preference these.
- Buy recycled products (like paper).
- Swap out your coffee for fair trade and use loose coffee options like French presses rather than pod coffee. Make sure products are from ethical and fairtrade sources.
- Buy reusable products that can have aspects replaced, such as refillable pens.
- Use whiteboards instead of paper and sticky notes, or find reusable options for single-use items.
- Replace single-use with reusable products wherever possible.
- Sell products no longer needed on the secondhand market or donate them to charity.
- Consider leasing or buying secondhand furniture and other supplies.
- Buy/lease green technology and use it for as long as possible.
- Find and offer repair services to keep products in use longer.
- Vet a list of ethical and sustainable catering suppliers; ensure all staff order from them.

WASTE

This applies to solid waste generated from offices, production processes and supply chains — although these are two very different types of waste. Let's start with office/building waste, as this is much easier to deal with.

Mostly you will have general waste (destined for landfill or incineration) and recycling (usually separated out into paper and plastics).

If you are more advanced, you will also have more granulated recycling (such as batteries and e-waste), along with organics for all your food waste.

As we have discussed before, recycling is a bit of a false positive, as the global recycling industry currently has many challenges. Many waste streams end up in landfill due to the lack of facilities to process it and the massive increase in production of plastic and paper waste.

Waste can also be trafficked, as is often the case with electronic waste. So, ensuring your waste managers have valid tracing and processing validation is very important.

The best waste policy is one of massive reduction in the generation of it. Double wins can be achieved here, as waste removal is often an expensive bottom line for organizations. So, the more you can reduce, the more cost savings you will have to invest in your sustainability initiatives. A waste audit (see next page) will help you get an idea of what is in your waste stream.

Waste generated at the factory and site level is much more complex to deal with since it can range from toxic sludge to offcuts or food waste. You will need to identify the types of waste generated, categorize them for safety and explore ways of dramatically reducing the waste generation at source.

ACTIONS TO TAKE:

- Implement organic recycling and make it enjoyable for staff to separate out food waste.
- Reduce the size of the general waste bins and remove waste bin liners.

OPERATIONS IMPACT ASSESSMENT TOOL: HOW TO DO AN OFFICE WASTE AUDIT

MATERIALS NEEDED

Personal protective gear (gloves, goggles, masks, etc.)
Large scale to weigh the waste
Tarpaulins or big washable sheets of plastic
Documentation tools
Appropriate places to store the waste

1. Set aside a specific time frame, such as 24 or 36 hours, where you will collect and assess all the waste produced from your site (ensure that the waste is stored and not discarded in this time period).

2. Once waste has been collected, find a location where you can make a mess (a car park is usually the best option). Then you will need to lay out your reusable plastic sheets or tarps, dump out the collected trash, photograph it and start to separate it. If you don't want to do that, then you can weigh and just visually document what is seen inside. But the idea here is to assess rates of contaminant and how much of your current landfill waste stream can be reduced or redirected.

   The goal is to get an idea of how much volume and weight of each type of waste is generated in a specific time period, along with the contents of that waste to see what could be reduced, changed, separated, etc.

3. If you are willing to separate it out, make a pile of organic waste and other different waste type piles, like potential recycling or items that should not be discarded at work!

4. Document with photos and size/weight of each section so that you can make some calculations on year-end costs and reduction options. The goal is to gain a clearer understanding of what is being discarded, what could be composted or recycled and what could have been reused.

5. Call your waste provider or look at your bills to see how much you are being charged for the different waste streams you have, and assign this to your waste audit.

6. You should then be able to estimate yearly costs in the current base case scenario and identify improvements that can be made through waste reduction, organic recycling and/or changes to procurement to alter the waste streams coming out of your office.

<table>
<tr><td>WASTE AUDIT</td><td>Use this waste audit to refine management and implement new procedures where gaps exist.</td></tr>
</table>

TRASH BINS IN YOUR FACILITY	**RECYCLING BINS IN YOUR FACILITY**	**ORGANIC WASTE BINS IN YOUR FACILITY**
# OF FLOORS	**# OF FLOORS**	**# OF FLOORS**
#OF BINS PER FLOOR	**#OF BINS PER FLOOR**	**#OF BINS PER FLOOR**
WEIGHT OR VOLUME OF EACH	**WEIGHT OR VOLUME OF EACH**	**WEIGHT OR VOLUME OF EACH**
TOTAL WEIGHT OR VOLUME	**TOTAL WEIGHT OR VOLUME**	**TOTAL WEIGHT OR VOLUME**

- Reuse before recycling wherever possible.
- Find ways of dramatically reducing printing, like setting printers to automatically print double-sided or moving to digital signing (however, you will need to check cloud storage impacts).
- Incentivize staff to reduce waste generation by assigning some metrics or targets per floor/group/team/etc.
- Assess your procurement contracts for unnecessary packaging/waste being purchased and anything else that can be reduced/removed.
- Provide good clear signage to communicate waste separation and goals.
- Develop a zero waste strategy that moves you to eliminate all waste from going to landfill.
- Find a second life for your waste.

TRANSPORTATION & TRAVEL

Your staff's transport options and your business's delivery services are two main transport considerations that you will need to assess. The location of your required place of work and the public transport options will affect the overall transport impacts you have related to your workers. Is it easy for staff to commute via mass transit or do they have to drive to get to work?

Explore the delivery methods used, number of flights taken by staff and general commuting practices of your workforce. Carbon emissions can be calculated for all of these, and policies that help reduce this impact area through behavior change can be implemented.

A lot has changed since COVID, so you may have already made drastic changes to your transport impact. Are staff taking fewer flights? Has video conferencing made it easier for people to work from home?

ACTIONS TO TAKE:

- Provide incentives for staff to commute in lower-impact ways, such as bike storage and repair, showers, changing rooms, transport cards, etc.
- Consider distributed work times to enable easier public transport commutes.
- Disincentivize driving by reducing car spaces.

- Provide technology that enables ride-sharing for staff.
- Purchase company electric vehicles.
- Increase technology that enables telecommuting.
- Use low-carbon delivery services like bike couriers.
- Make it easier for staff to fly less by providing desirable technology that makes it easy to connect with clients.
- Offer rewards for staff who fly less (consider an UnFrequent Flyers Club!).
- When booking flights, support companies with environmental policies, take direct flights and combine trips to reduce unnecessary flights.
- If you have to fly, offset it in validated ways.
- Select hotels and accommodation services that have environmental performance standards and actively work to reduce their impacts (like green key hotels).

INFRASTRUCTURE

Every sector has a different set of infrastructures that they are responsible for managing; thus, they will have a different set of considerations that they need to work through to ensure that the environmental performance is operating effectively.

For buildings and manufacturing sites, this would be mostly due to internal temperature maintenance through heating and cooling, the amount of energy used to operate the facility, along with the inputs and outputs generated through operations and how they are managed on site.

Things like wastewater filtration systems, on-site renewable energy, organic material composting or other forms of bioremediation and solar passive heating and cooling all dramatically reduce infrastructure impacts. There are several types of building designs that also allow for a significant reduction in operational impacts, and retrofitting existing infrastructure can create financial savings.

ACTIONS TO TAKE:

- Optimize heating and cooling systems to minimize energy use and add insulation to reduce heat loss.

- Ensure all outputs are managed, like air filtration systems.
- Install low-energy systems optimized to take advantage of airflow and sunlight.
- Consider how people move around your building and look for lower energy options like stairs over elevators where accessibility allows.
- Set up a compost system, worm farm or compost collection service for organic waste.
- Introduce plants and living things to purify air and offer biophilic experiences.
- Install behavior-changing features that communicate low-energy use.
- Offer reusable options on site.
- Regularly service, maintain and repair equipment to reduce the need to replace.

3.3 PRODUCT LEVEL IMPACTS

Product level impacts cover all aspects of the produced products and services created by the company as part of their offering into the economy. It doesn't matter if the product is an app or the phone that the app runs on; everything can be assessed for its impact in creation, delivery, use and end of life.

All goods that are created rely on materials extracted from nature and exist within a complex global supply chain that has impacts at multiple stages. By assessing products across their entire life cycle from the extraction of raw materials through to the end of life, you get a far more detailed and accurate perspective of where impacts are occurring so that they can then be redesigned.

Changes to product design and service delivery decisions should be implemented to ensure that supply chains and auxiliary aspects of company production activities have been considered in line with reducing and avoiding negative consequences.

Once full life cycle and supply chain impacts are understood, then sustainable design strategies can be employed. Let's get started by understanding how to explore the current linear economy by looking at the life cycle stages that a product goes through.

THE 5 MAIN LIFE CYCLE STAGES

Everything that is produced goes through these five main life cycle stages: material extraction, manufacturing, packaging and transportation, use and end of life (EOL).

At each of these stages, there are inputs and outputs, flow-throughs, value losses and potential gains. In Life Cycle Thinking (LCT), we use these as a foundation for thinking through what needs to happen in order for something to be made so that we can redesign the functional delivery as part of a circular and sustainable model.

1. MATERIAL EXTRACTION

Everything comes from nature at some point, so all materials can be traced back to where and how they were extracted. Whether they have been pulled out of the ground, cut down, or shorn off a sheep's back, their extraction affects nature. When we take from the planet, we change and often destroy ecosystems that might otherwise have been providing valuable ecosystem services. This is called land use changes. Many current extraction processes are destructive rather than regenerative and the change to land use can have far reaching system impacts.

For example, the most biodiverse place on the planet, the Amazon Rainforest, is being cleared at an unprecedented rate to grow soy to feed cattle to meet the growing global demand for cheap meat products. Likewise, the demand for hard wood timbers drives the cleaning of old growth forests and these are replaced with palm plantations to meet the need for cheap lubricants such as palm oil. Rainforest ecosystems are critical for climate and food security.

From a life cycle perspective, we always go back to what the land was being used for before we extracted the materials and then evaluate the method of extraction. Often, an ecosystem service was being provided by nature for free but is no longer able to occur as a result of the extraction.

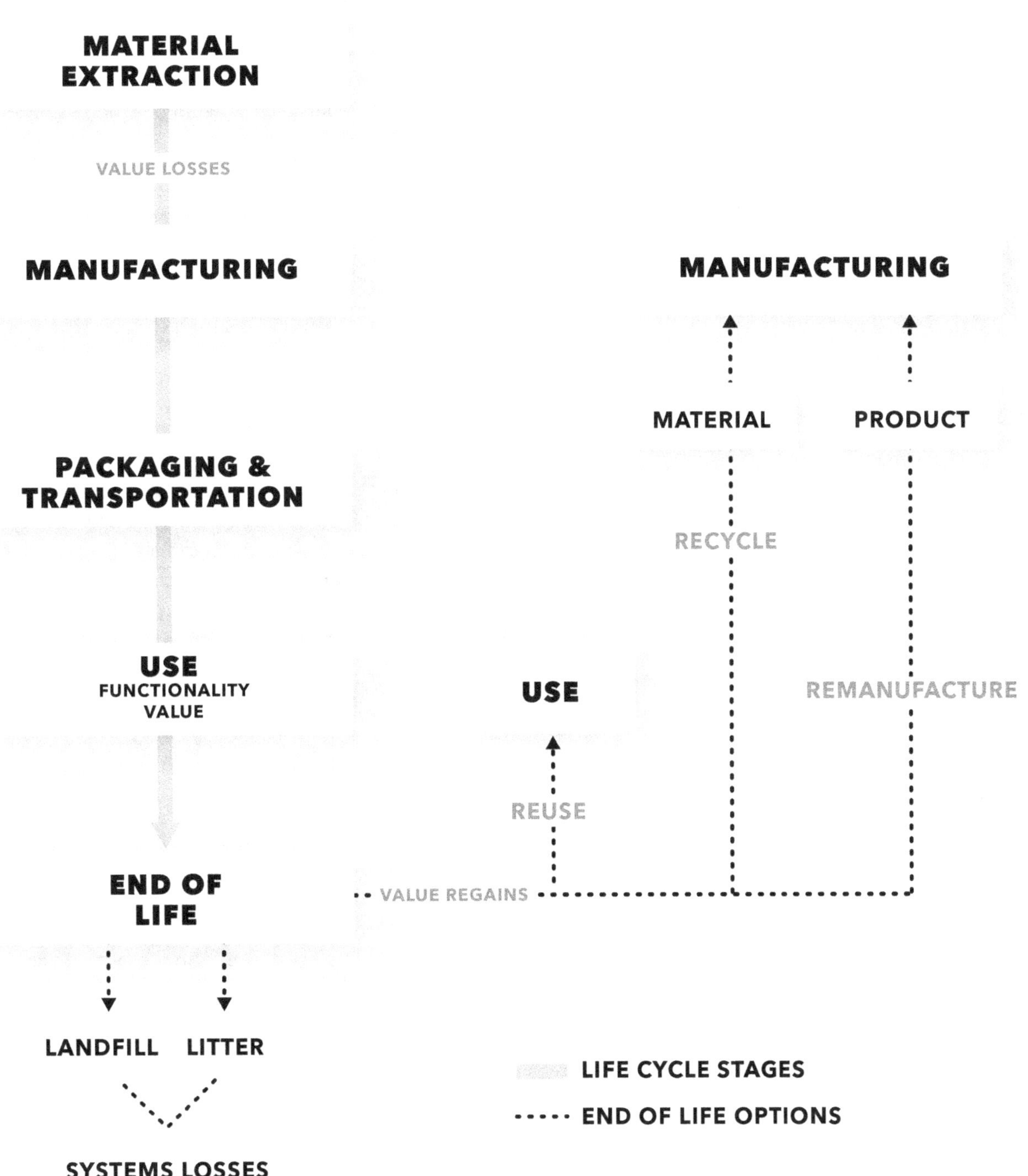
MATERIAL
EXTRACTION
VALUE LOSSES
MANUFACTURING
PACKAGING &
TRANSPORTATION
USE
FUNCTIONALITY
VALUE
END OF
LIFE
LANDFILL
LITTER
SYSTEMS LOSSES
MANUFACTURING
MATERIAL
PRODUCT
RECYCLE
REMANUFACTURE
USE
REUSE
VALUE REGAINS
LIFE CYCLE STAGES
END OF LIFE OPTIONS

2. MANUFACTURING

This is where we take the extracted materials and transform them into usable materials, products and goods. For example, a tree is turned into wood chips, bleached and chemically separated, heat rolled, made into paper, and then lined with a plastic film and turned into a coffee cup. Petroleum oil is refined into different chemicals that can then be made into plastic pellets and extracted into bags.

Activities in the manufacturing stage must be accounted for, with the inputs and outputs being identified and explored for their positive and negative impacts. In the tree example above, the inputs would be energy and trees, and the outputs would be CO2, sawdust and paper.

In doing a life cycle exploration, it helps to start by writing a bill of materials that for the product and then backtrack on how they are made and extracted.

3. PACKAGING AND TRANSPORTATION

This happens at every stage of the product's life and is often where people assume the biggest ecological impacts occur — but that isn't necessarily the case, especially if you look at all the activities across the entire life of the product.

Packaging is a real conundrum, as it's often overdone, using materials that don't return to nature well. However, from a life cycle perspective, sometimes the loss of the product is greater than the loss of the packaging. For example, loose leaf salad greens — if they are packed in a plastic bag, we often have considerably less product loss. Ecologically speaking, this is the better option. But the bags are often unrecyclable and destined for landfill, where they don't do much. However, if they end up in nature, they cause havoc. These are the types of tradeoffs that must be navigated using a full systems perspective.

Transport is much the same; sometimes it makes sense to transport things across the world rather than grow them locally if the climate conditions do not allow for it. Tomatoes being shipped from a warmer location are often more environmentally friendly than those grown in a hothouse in a cold climate using fossil fuel inputs.

Packaging and transportation are tricky parts of a product's life cycle and require considerable expertise and examination if they are to be understood. Thankfully there has been a lot of work done on this stage, and plenty of published data can be reviewed for consideration. There are also several online life cycle assessment tool, especially for packaging assessment.

4. USE PHASE

This is where we buy the product, take it home, plug it in, use it, maybe wash it or perhaps add extra things to it. Products that require use phase additions (like power or cleaning) are called active products, while those that don't need anything to operate during the use phase (like a chair) are passive products.

 Active products often have a high impact during the use phase because they constantly draw from other systems. Use phase impacts can also be determined by the behaviors of the customer, such as overfilling an electric kettle and thus wasting energy. Or the system will dictate the use impact, such as what energy sources are available to wash a pair of jeans or charge a product.

5. END OF LIFE

The end-of-life impacts vary dramatically based on the options available in the end location and the way the product was designed.

You may recall that there are four main EOL options:
* Landfill (we lose value from the system and create negative externalities)
* Littering (we lose value from the system and create negative externalities)
* Recycling (with degrees of remanufacturing, reuse, repair, etc.)
* Incineration (replaces some fossil fuel production, but we lose the materials from the system)

Each option has its own degree of impact (and emotional triggers!). Many people hate waste and therefore assume that the end of life is the biggest part of a product's impact. But in a lot of cases, it's not.

Despite saying this, it is incredibly important to recognize that all waste is a tragedy, as it is a loss that has to be replaced from nature. Most human-designed systems lose value over time, so we end up with built-in wastefulness through disposability. All EOL issues must be addressed at the start of the product's life, not the end.

When assessing a current product design, use percentages to estimate the likelihood of where a product's end of life destiny is, based on the current circumstances. For example, a pen is very unlikely to be recycled (5%), highly likely to be lost (25%), most likely ending up in landfill (70%).

LIFE CYCLE THINKING KEY CONCEPTS

As we discussed in Part 1 (see page 63), Life Cycle Thinking is based off of the methodology of product environmental impact assessment called Life Cycle Assessment, which is the scientific process of

understanding the impacts that occur as a result of the products that move through our economy.

There are several key concepts that apply to both the more technical assessment process and the streamlined thinking tool explored here.

CONTEXT: The conditions in which the product will exist such as the climate, use case, durability, repair options, cultural norms, energy sources, etc. will all determine the life cycle impacts, so always consider the contextual scenarios and conditions to get the full picture.

FUNCTIONAL UNIT: Defining the product's performance criteria, such as how much liquid a cup can hold or if something has to conduct electricity, or even the amount of calories delivered by a type of food, allows for things that are of the same functionality to be compared. Everything that is sold in the economy has a definable functional unit — that is the unit of functional delivery.

INPUTS: Everything that is created requires things to come from nature. These are essentially the inputs, which are the resources that are required in order for a change to happen, such as a chicken

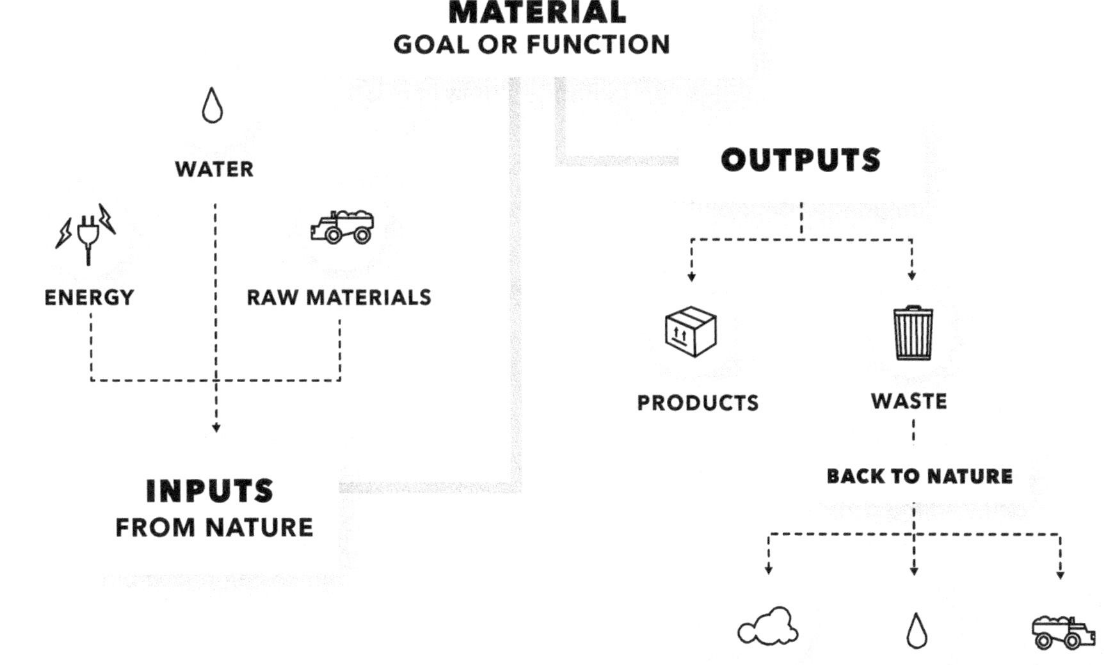

PRODUCT IMPACT ASSESSMENT TOOL: HOW TO DO A LIFE CYCLE MAP

MATERIALS NEEDED

Large pieces of paper
Different colored pens and markers

Life cycle mapping is a discovery tool that empowers more detailed reflection on cause and effect while also offering fascinating insights that can dramatically change the way you produce and deliver a product to market.

The purpose of life cycle mapping is to explore and compare the impacts of the entire life of a product, especially to understand the current linear process it goes through.

You can create quick maps, which give you a basic perspective, or spend more time developing a detailed understanding of all the inputs and outputs that go into making something exist. However you approach this, creating a map will help you uncover a set of incredibly useful new insights that lead to circular and sustainable design opportunities. Here's how to get started:

1. Start by defining what you are going to explore, whether it's a product or material. If you want to compare different things, you must define the functional unit, which often involves defining its core purpose.

   For example, a cup of hot liquid requires you to use different materials and physical properties than a cup that holds cold liquid, so you need to understand the purpose of the thing in order to understand what its function is.

2. Once you have defined the scope of your exploration, grab a piece of paper (use the template provided on the previous page) and add the five main life cycle stages as headings so you can start to map against them.

3. Identify the main ingredients/materials used so you can explore the material extraction phase by identifying all the things that have to happen in order to get the raw materials out of nature.

   This can be quite detailed for complex products (like a cell phone that has 50 different materials in it), but you have your general knowledge and the internet to figure these things out!

   It helps to do an online search to identify the main materials and the processes used to make them; then, draw links between how the material is made (in the manufacturing stage) and how it was extracted from nature.

4. Extracted materials are then processed into usable goods (such as iron ore into a usable metal), so you document each material's manufacturing processes. Explore the stages they go through in order to go from raw to usable state, the inputs that are required and the outputs that come about as a result.

   For example, there are many different ways of transforming bamboo into a usable industrial material. If it's used for something like a spoon, there will be far fewer manufacturing stages than if it is turned into a fabric, which often requires many chemical processes.

You can discover many of these things with a quick internet search to help build your knowledge bank on material processing.

5. The raw materials are then combined to make the usable good, which is also documented in the manufacturing phase.

6. Now you can start to explore the other phases of the product's life, such as packaging and transportation. How are the extracted materials packaged and transported around the world? What is the usable good delivered to market in?

7. Move onto the use phase next, where you consider all the different use-case scenarios that are likely to occur. Is the product active or passive? What are the use phase inputs, such as water for washing or energy for charging?

Try to calculate what a functional unit's use impact is, meaning if you want to get one cup of boiled water, how much energy is required for an electric kettle, a stove top pot heated by electric or gas or an instant water boiler?

It's here in the use phase that you will notice just how much the design decisions influence the impacts of the product during its usable life. The use phase can include the retail and sales environment as well, but often the main impacts occur in the relationship between the design and the human interaction with it.

8. After use, map the potential EOL options and again draw links between the materials used and the most likely ways they would be discarded. You will find that the way things are assembled often directly impacts the ways they are treated at their end of life. For example, some cell phones are designed to intentionally lock the consumer out with special patented screw heads, yet they will have a warning about not disposing of the battery in the normal trash — even though you can't get into the phone to remove the battery!

Consider what the most likely EOL scenarios are, like recycling, reuse, or remanufacturing. Not everyone will recycle, some products get lost through litter, and not all cities offer comprehensive recycling schemes!

Also, be sure to check whether something really is recyclable. Paper cups, for example, are not recyclable, as they are lined with a plastic film that makes it very hard to get value out of the recycling process. Again, this stage will help you appreciate just how much the initial design affects what happens to the product.

When completed, your map should give you a broader perspective of the life cycle implications and offer insights into areas of redesign and improvement.

<table>
<tr><td>LIFE CYCLE MAPPING</td><td>Use this worksheet as a guide to mapping out your product's life cycle stages.</td></tr>
</table>

EXTRACTION

WHICH RAW MATERIALS ARE NEEDED, AND WHERE DO THEY COME FROM?

MANUFACTURING

HOW ARE THE MATERIALS AND FINAL PRODUCT MADE?

PACKAGING & TRANSPORT

HOW ARE PRODUCTS PROTECTED, AND HOW ARE THEY MOVING AROUND?

USE PHASE

HOW ARE THE PRODUCTS BEING USED, AND ARE THEY ACTIVE OR PASSIVE?

Active products need inputs to work, e.g., charging a phone. Passive products don't need inputs to work, e.g., a chair.

END OF LIFE OPTIONS

WHERE DO THE PRODUCTS END UP, AFTER HOW LONG, AND FOR HOW LONG?

being grown for meat or water being used to grow plants as food stock to grow the chicken.

There are a bazillion different types of inputs, but think of it this way: to get something out, we must put something in - raw materials, energy, water, chemicals, etc.

Inputs can all be traced back to nature at some point, so we need to understand what impact their extraction has had on the resilience of natural systems.

OUTPUTS: These are the intended and unintended results of processing inputs. Water coming into a factory can help to break up wood fiber to make paper, but it also creates contaminated wastewater due to the chemicals used in the processing. This should be treated before re-entering the natural environment, which will also have outputs. A chicken farm has the outputs of manure that, if untreated, can have adverse human health and environmental impacts, such as contributing to dead zones in the oceans from nutrient increases.

Outputs are all the pollutants, byproducts, and actual intended products which occur when we process something.

FLOW-THROUGH: This is the way things flow through a system from input to output, along with the activities that occur throughout. We call this "stocks and flows" in systems thinking, and it results in feedback loops. In LCT, it helps to think about how things flow through the system in order to get to the desired outcome at each stage of the product's life.

GOAL AND SCOPE: The goal is the delivery of the functional unit, and the scope is the framing that the LCA study is done through.

LCA GOAL & SCOPE

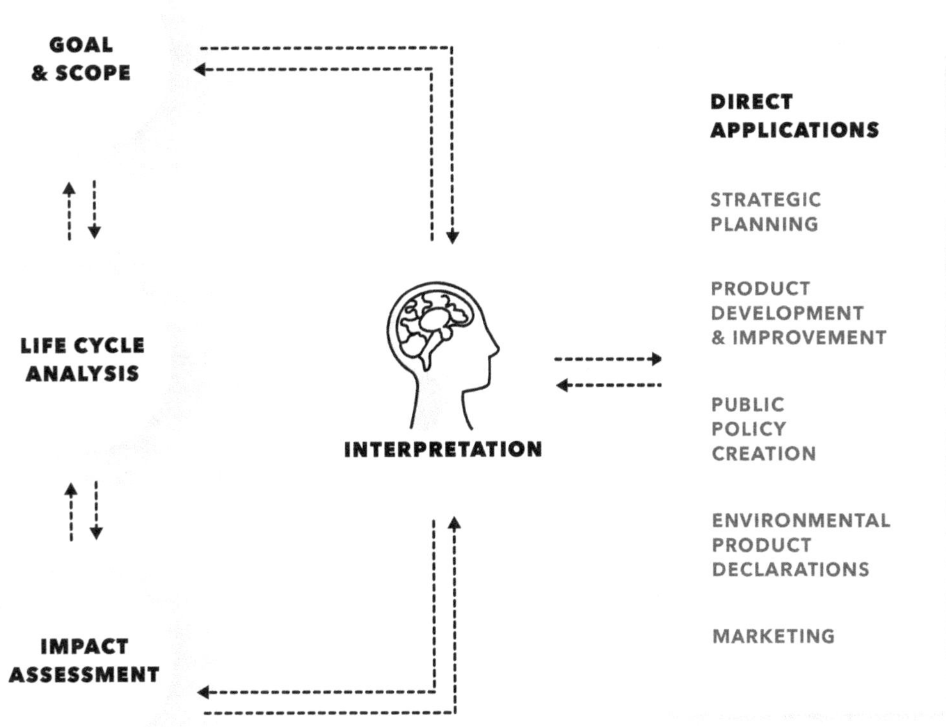

ADAPTED FROM THE EN ISO 14040

The scope outlines what is included in the assessment and what is excluded. For example, if you had a study that only compared the impacts of a large family restaurant chain inside the restaurant walls (e.g., cooking and waste) but ignored the meat production, packaging and all other inputs needed to function as a food provider, then the study would not be a proper LCA, as it needs to cover the full scope of delivering the products to the customer.

METABOLISM RATE: The ability for things to be reabsorbed or integrated into a system, be it biological or industrial, describes the metabolism rate. Food waste, for example, can be easily metabolized in a compost bin or biodigester, whereas it does not get effectively metabolized in a landfill.

IMPACTS: Everything that is created requires something else to be altered, destroyed, converted, etc. Actions result in reactions and consequences, and in life cycle thinking and sustainability in general, we are concerned with the impacts of actions.

If you are deciding whether to swap your packaging from one material to another, you need to think about the resulting impacts across the life of the product.

How do you maximize the functional gain, while minimizing inputs and the negative outputs on people, the planet and the bottom line?

SUPPLY CHAIN ASSESSMENT

Your supply chain will be filled with different processes, materials, and providers. Being able to map all of these activities along the value chain is

MANAGING SUPPLY CHAIN IMPACTS ACROSS THE FULL LIFE CYCLE

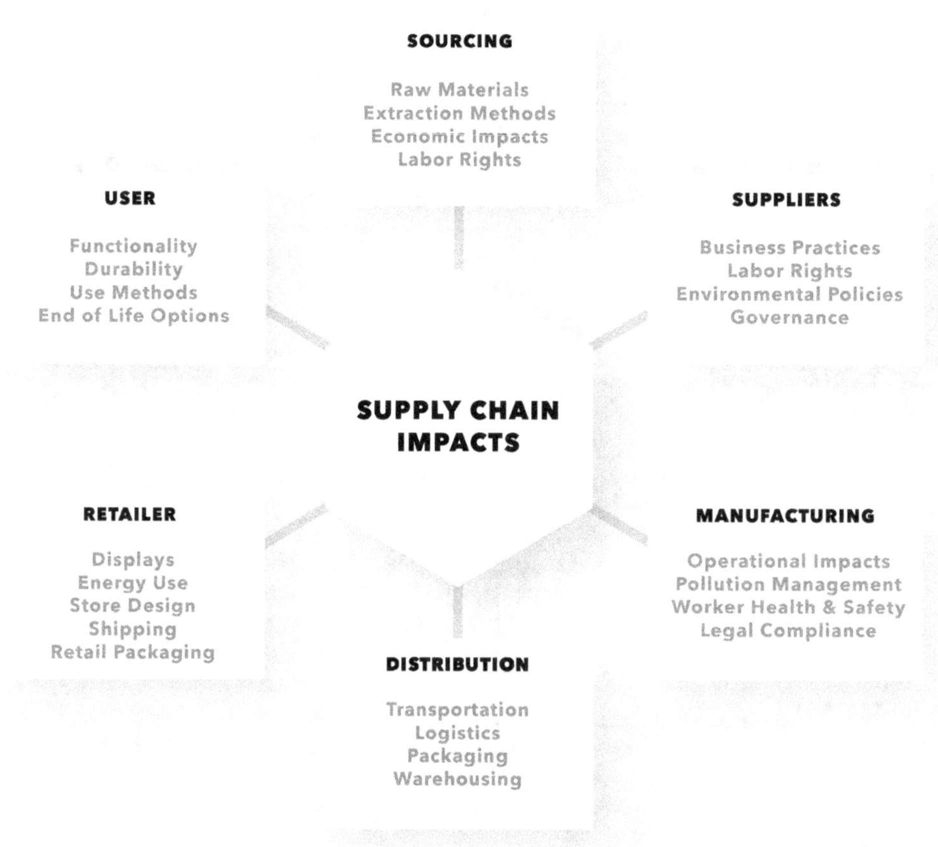

crucial in understanding where impacts are occurring and in taking steps to reduce, mitigate or eliminate them. This is especially the case when it comes to social sustainability.

Supply chains cover the flow of materials through organizations, people, activities, information and resources involved in getting a product to an end consumer.

Whatever product or service you offer, you are involved in supply chains.

By understanding where you fit within the flow of goods, the impacts that occur at different stages and which ones can be attributed to your product, you can make changes that reduce impacts.

One universal aspect of supply chains is that they are complex, which can make it difficult to understand all the many stages that a product moves through. The best way to overcome this is through supply chain mapping.

This is where the activities of actors along a supply chain are mapped through all stages, from transformation of natural resources into raw materials through to manufacturing, distribution and delivery of finished product to market.
This is different to life cycle thinking, as LCT maps don't tend to include social impacts.

SUPPLY CHAIN CONSIDERATIONS:

- What are all the stages your product goes through before it gets to you?
- Where are materials coming from, and how are the people extracting them working?
- Where is the energy being sourced from, and where can you shift from fossil to renewable fuel sources?
- What are the hidden impacts embedded within the supply chain, such as slavery in agriculture or mining?
- How can you recover and put to good use all wasted resources across the supply chain? Are there ways of partnering to create industrial symbiosis in which your product's by-products are used as raw materials for another process?
- How is waste managed from industrial processes? Is it dumped or sold off?

- Reduce waste to landfill by encouraging secondary industries to use industrial by-products.
- Do you need to produce a product to deliver the functional unit? Look for alternative business models to deliver your customer's functional desires.
- Are your suppliers using ethical and fair labor practices? How do you validate this?
- What are the outputs from each of the main stages of your supply chain; are these being managed effectively?
- Where are your raw materials being sourced from? Are there any ethical/environmental issues in this (such as illegal hard woods)?
- Which third-party services can be used to validate your suppliers?
- How can you promote transparency along your supply chain?

SUPPLY CHAIN WASTE

Supply chain waste is complex since much of the waste generated will be outside of your direct control, which makes it hard to assess and manage. Often there are hundreds of steps that a product goes through before it ends up in your hands.

Regardless, if you are responsible for the creation of that product or you are the purchaser of it for your company's use, then you should attempt to find the most waste-efficient solution to creation and delivery into the market.

ACTIONS TO TAKE:

- Ask suppliers to reduce packaging for office and catering supplies.
- Buy in bulk to reduce individual packaging on products.
- Combine orders to reduce boxing, etc.
- Check with providers to see if they have environmental policies and what actions they are taking.
- Reuse packaging that enters your facility to pack your own goods in.
- Require suppliers to agree to your waste and sustainability policy as well as make changes to adhere to it.
- Find the optimal amount of packaging needed to protect without wasting.

UNITED NATIONS GLOBAL COMPACT

The United Nations set up the Global Compact (globalreporting.org), which promotes sustainable supply chain management. The Global Compact is a non-binding pact calling on companies to take action for the Sustainable Development Goals (SDGs) and has 10 key principles, including human rights, labor rights, the environment, anti-corruption and more.

Organizations that join the Global Compact are expected to adhere to these 10 principles in their daily operations, organizational culture and overarching corporate strategies. These should align with their company's value system and approach to doing business.

Supply chain sustainability is the first step in addressing the product-level impact of your organization. It offers full-spectrum management of the goods and services that go into and come out of your supply chain. This is also critical for addressing Scope 3 Emissions under the Greenhouse Gas Protocol.

THE 10 PRINCIPLES OF THE UN GLOBAL COMPACT SUPPLY CHAINS & PROCUREMENT STRATEGIES TO INTEGRATE SUSTAINABILITY

HUMAN RIGHTS

1. Businesses should support and respect the protection of internationally proclaimed human rights

2. Make sure they are not complicit in human rights abuses

LABOR

3. Businesses should uphold the freedom of association and the effective recognition of the right to collective bargaining

4. The elimination of all forms of forced and compulsory labor

5. The effective abolition of child labor

6. The elimination of discrimination in respect of employment and occupation

ENVIRONMENT

7. Businesses should support a precautionary approach to environmental challenges

8. Undertake initiatives to promote greater environmental responsibility

9. Encourage the development and diffusion of environmentally friendly technologies

ANTI CORRUPTION

10. Businesses should work against corruption in all its forms, including extortion and bribery

Source: unglobalcompact.org

- Offer take-back and reuse programs for your customers or use suppliers who offer this.
- Find partners to use your production waste or ensure that it is effectively recycled on site.
- Look for secondary uses for your waste products; examples include bread being made into beer or grape skins from wine production being made into cattle feed.
- Select materials that can be benignly digested back into nature and ensure industrial composting for collection.

MATERIAL SELECTION

Different materials have different impacts throughout their life. The way they are made, the end of life options, the many different combinations and how they are transformed into a product will all greatly affect the overall impact of the material choices. Think about how much energy is needed to make aluminium, but then how light it is, so how much energy it can save in use.

It's important to understand these different performance aspects of a material and consider potential impact areas of each material from a holistic standpoint since each material has varying degrees of impacts at different stages of their life. This will help you make a more informed decision about which material will both meet your needs from a functional standpoint and have the right EOL option when disposed of.

The hardest thing is often the trade-offs in decision making that need to be made. All materials have impacts, with some being far greater than others in their extraction and manufacturing stage and others being greater at the end of life.

The impact is not embedded in the material itself; it's what you do with it coupled with the way you design the product and business model that will determine how big an impact it has. For example, plastics are not inherently bad; it's the application of them in single-use scenarios that determines the degree of impact. Likewise, the use of glass packaging might seem better, but in fact, it has a higher embodied energy in production and in recycling, and we are running out of sand to make glass.

SUSTAINABLE DESIGN STRATEGIES

Circular and sustainable design is all about transforming your product and experiences into a waste and impact-free outcome. It requires reimagining not only the product design and materials used, but also an entirely new business model that eliminates single-use materials and introduces services that cycle products around again and again.

The concept of designing products and services to have the lowest possible impact on the planet has been developing across industry for over 50 years. There are a series of tried and tested strategies that help reduce material and life-cycle impacts, as well as new strategies for transforming businesses into circular companies.

Strategies are best fitted to your specific needs and include approaches like the following curated list of "Design for X" Strategies. These approaches all consider the circular economy and how they relate to closing the loop as well as dramatically changing economic models.

In order to achieve sustainable and circular design, some (or many) of these design considerations need to be employed in combination throughout the design process in order to ensure that the outcome is not just a reinterpretation of the status quo, but something that actually challenges and changes the way we meet our needs.

DEMATERIALIZATION: Reducing the overall size, weight and number of materials incorporated into a design is a simple way of keeping down the environmental impact if you don't lose quality and thus reduce lifespan.

LONGEVITY: Increasing the lifespan of the products through material selection, repair options and resell value, done by creating products that are aesthetically timeless, highly durable and able to retain their value over time so people can resell them or pass them on.

MODULARITY: Products that can be reconfigured in different ways to adapt to different spaces and uses. Modularity as a sustainable design approach implicates the end owner in the design so that they can reconfigure the product to fit their changing life needs or it can include add-ons from the producer to increase longevity.

DISASSEMBLY: Designing a product so that it can be very easily taken apart for recycling and remanufacturing at the end of its life or be taken back and reconditioned by the producer. How it's put together, the types of materials used and the connection methods all need to be designed to increase the speed and ease of taking it apart for repair, remanufacturing and recycling.

RECYCLABILITY: Making a recyclable product goes beyond simply selecting a material that can be recycled. You have to consider the recyclability of all the materials, the way they are put together and the use case, along with the ease of recycling at end of life in the location that it will be used.

REPAIRABILITY: Repair is a fundamental aspect of the circular economy. Things wear out, break, get damaged, and need to be designed to allow for easy repair, upgrading, and fixability. Along with the extra parts and instructions on how to do this, we need systems that support repair in society, rather than discourage it.

REUSABILITY: Repair allows the end owner to maintain its value over time or to sell it more easily to then increase its lifespan. But there is also the option of designing so that the product can be reused in a different way from its intended original purpose without much extra material or energy inputs. An example of this is a condiment jar designed to be used as a water glass, or the owner of the product takes it back and reuses it again.

REMANUFACTURING: This is when a product is not completely disassembled and recycled or reused, but instead, some parts are designed to be reconfigured and other parts recycled, depending on what wears out and what maintains its usefulness over time. This requires the producer to take the product back or work with third parties to enable the remanufacture.

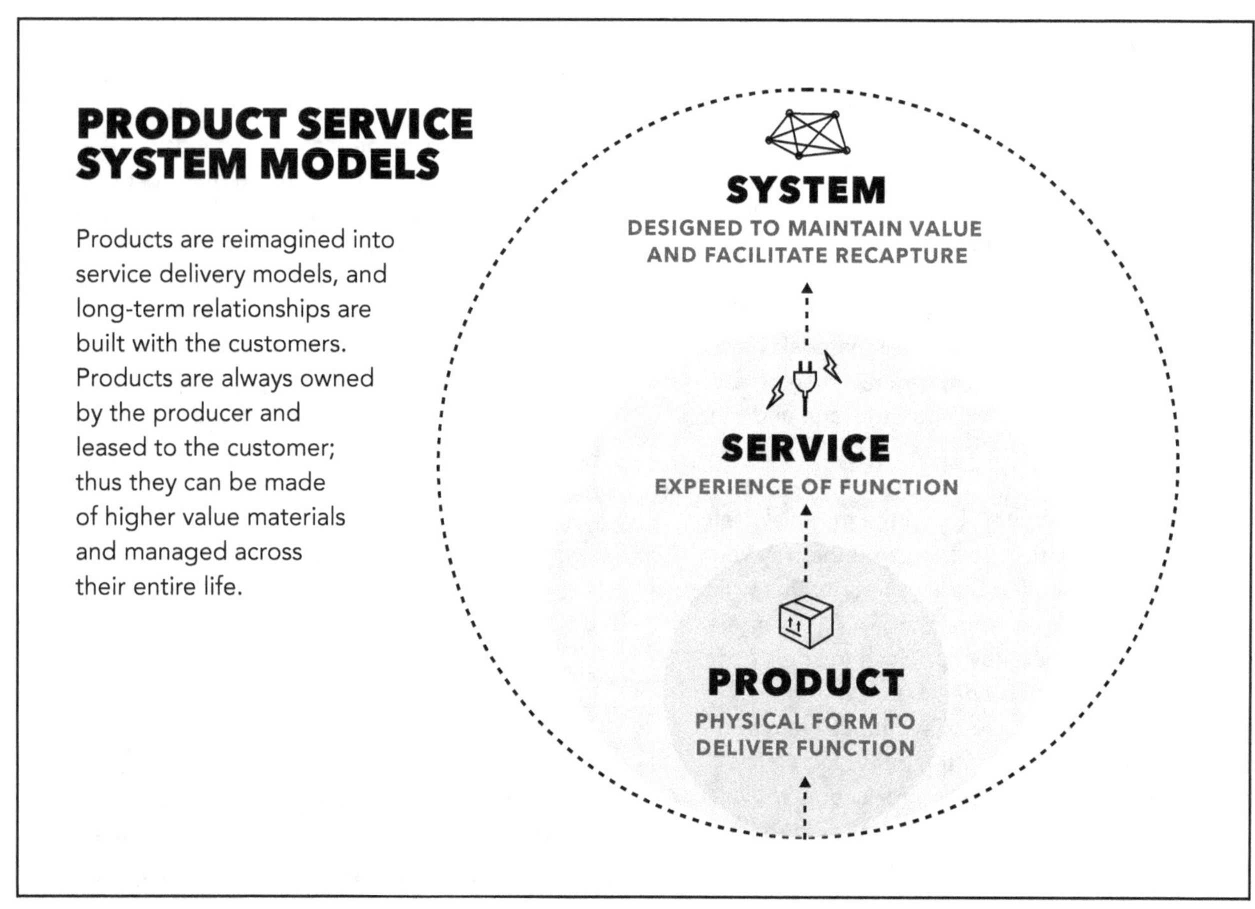

EFFICIENCY: During the use phase, many products require constant inputs like energy. Active products that constantly tap into other active systems to achieve function create scope for inefficiency. Design for efficiency dramatically reduces the input requirements of the product during its use phase, increases the environmental performance and reduces wear of the product, increasing lifetime use.

INFLUENCE: The things we design in turn design us, and thus there is a huge scope for creating products, services, and systems that influence society in more positive ways. There is still a lot of resistance to sustainability, often because it seems confusing or requires work. So, imagine how you can design things that give people an alternative experience to this mainstream perspective.

EQUITY: Accidentally or intentionally, many goods are designed to reinforce stereotypes, like pink toys for girls, and chunky watches for men. Reinforcing stereotypes subtly maintains negative and inequitable status quos in society. Design for equity requires the reflection and disruption of the mainstream references that reinforce inequitable access to resources, be it based on gender, different ability access or outdated stereotypes.

PRODUCTS AS SERVICES: One of the main approaches to enacting the circular economy is to change the way products move through the economy so that instead of them ending up as waste, they are designed to be reused and cycled round and round intentionally-designed closed-loop systems. This is called a Product Service System model or "Products as Services".

In this approach, products are owned by the producer and leased to the customer; therefore they can be made of higher value materials and managed across their entire life. The producer designs the takeback and redeployment system that enables the customer to have a seamless experience and the producer to cycle the products round and round the system with minimal waste.

SYSTEMS CHANGE: Perhaps the most important of the design strategy tools is the ability to design interventions that actively shift the status quo of an unsustainable or inequitable system. The world is made up of systems, and everything we do will have an impact in some way on the systems around us. Instead of seeing your product as an individual unit, see it as an animated agent in a system, interacting with other agents and thus having impacts.

ECOLABELS

After doing the work of creating more sustainable products, you may want to pursue ecolabels for your packaging or even consider a general certification, like a B Corp Certification. Obtaining these can be a complex process, so the overview below gives a starting point to help you think about what is right for you and how you may want to showcase your sustainability efforts.

There are three different types of ecolabels according to the ISO standard:

TYPE 1: These are the classic ecolabels that evaluate environmental product performance compared with other products that have the same function; they are considered the gold standard for consumer information because there is an independent certifying body.

TYPE 2: These are claims made by manufacturers, distributors, importers and retailers about the environmental aspects of their products or services. These claims are often more ambiguous.

TYPE 3: These are voluntary declarations around the sustainability of a product or service based on the entire life cycle. No certification is issued; instead, declarations are made.

Environmental Product Declarations (EPDs) are the environmental equivalent of technical specifications, and there are benefits to investing in them:

- Market Differentiation: EPDs help you define your product in the market and allow you to determine your product's environmental performance compared to your competitors.

- Customer Confidence: By having an EPD, you show your customers that you care about the environment and are willing to do the work to create a sustainable product.

- Legal and Regulatory Requirements: In some countries, public procurement bodies (such as in the EU) require EPDs to assess the environmental impact of products.

BENEFIT CORPORATIONS

Otherwise known as B Corp, in order to integrate social (and now environmental) responsibility into the DNA of a company, there are two methods of gaining B Corporation status. First is the certification provided by the B Corp organization, which involves a rigorous process of assessment and action.

The second is legally registering a company as a For Benefit Corporation in the company's constitution (Kickstarter is an example of a company that changed its constitution to be For Benefit). This option is currently only available in parts of the United States, Canada and the United Kingdom. As an approach to corporate governance, B Corp status is often motivated by the changing ethical landscape, whereby many stakeholders are requiring corporations to be active corporate citizens as well as service and product providers.

The difference between being certified B-Corp and being a For Benefit Corporation is a bit confusing. Basically, if a company has the Certified B Corp logo, they have obtained a third-party certification administered by the non-profit B Lab (www.bcorporation.net) that is based on their assessment criteria. The B Corporation logo and certification has become a respectable ecolabel that provides assessment of validity of the social and environmental impacts of the company who has obtained it.

In contrast, a For Benefit Corporation is a legal structure that exists in some parts of the world. This structure enables companies to operate as a type of hybrid between profit and not for profit, with constitutional validation of the beneficial role to society they are committed to.

3.4 EXPERIENTIAL IMPACTS

Experiential impacts are the outcome of the services, company culture and customer-facing offerings that your organization creates and fosters

"Certified B Corporations are a new kind of business that balances purpose and profit. They are legally required to consider the impact of their decisions on their workers, customers, suppliers, community, and the environment. This is a community of leaders, driving a global movement of people using business as a force for good."

- B Corporation Certification

with customers, suppliers and employees.

This is all about the interface you have with the world. The general areas of impact are around what the workforce is encouraged or discouraged to do, be it in how they get to work, the waste management on site, resource efficiency and general culture and company ethics. Then there is the customer journey and how people engage with your company, products and services.

Given that much of the circular economy is about designing closed-loop systems that have a high level of customer interaction, the experiential side of your offerings is crucial to your success. Additionally, the experiences of all players along your value chain will impact how effectively you create an ethical and sustainable company.

The experiences that you offer your customers and team members will impact their understanding of your organization and its ethos; in turn, it will affect their behaviors. By considering and designing experiences that affect positive change, challenging unsustainable cultural norms and offering entirely new ways of delivering value into the economy, you can embed sustainability into your workforce and wider value-chain.

The six areas that we explore in customer and staff sustainability experiences are:

JOURNEY: The way your customer interacts with all your offerings, such as how they move through your space, interact with your website or return

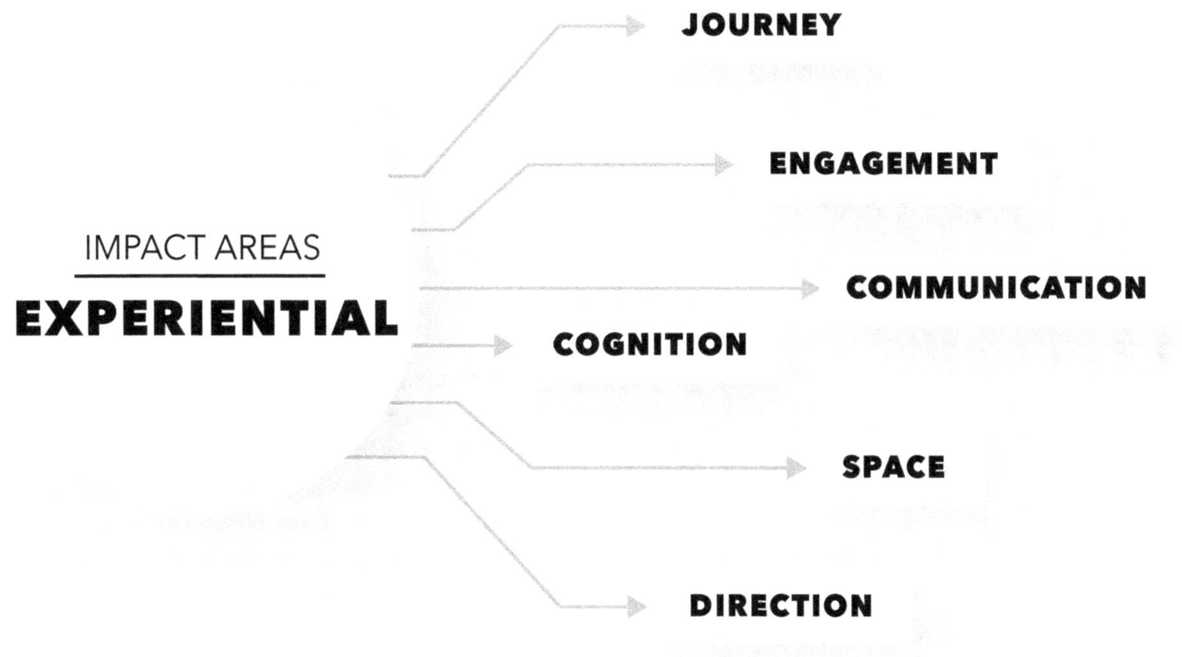

your product when no longer needed as part of a product as service model. All journeys have multiple touchpoints that could be contributing to unsustainability or adjusted to promote sustainable actions.

ENGAGEMENT: This is how you engage your customer, employees and stakeholders along your value chain. From communication to education, how you engage with the world determines how you are valued.

COMMUNICATION: There are many ways you can communicate with your customers, including brand identity and packaging designs, wayfinding signs that help direct them to better behaviors and even the emails that you send them. All the aspects of engagement could accidentally be encouraging unsustainable actions, or conversely, be redesigned to offer more encouragement and direction. The way you frame the offerings, the language you use and your approach will determine how willing people are to engage with your offerings.

COGNITION: This is how you understand and enhance the cognitive experience your customers have through the design, experience flow and behavioral insights associated with their cognitive experience of what you offer. Overcoming biases, ensuring that the experience is joyful, frictionless, incentivizing and rewarding — the cognitive experience design will greatly affect their behavior, perception and how likely a customer is to invest in your offering as well as how ethical and equitable the experience can become.

SPACE: This is about considering the physical spaces you design and how they influence your customers and workers throughout you facilities. Consider your offices and their layout, the way people move through a shop or cafe that you own — these will all impact their emotions, experiences, behaviors and willingness to participate in changes you make as part of your sustainability initiative.

DIRECTION: This is about how you guide social norms, behaviors, and culture by pro-actively encouraging customers and your team to do something sustainable, like bringing in their own coffee cup, refilling a water bottle, ordering differently, etc. You can help direct people to more sustainable offerings by designing the experience to maximize these preferences and reducing friction that adopting new norms could result in.

At every stage of your customer journey, you can design both the physical and cognitive experiences to nudge and direct people toward better preferences and choices that lead to more sustainable outcomes.

EXPERIENCE DESIGN

Experience design is the process of enhancing stakeholder satisfaction by improving the usability, accessibility and pleasure provided in the interaction between the user and the product, and more broadly, the interaction with a company.

Most of our lives are defined by the experiences we have with the world around us — the physical spaces we move through, the websites we engage with, the products we use for work and leisure. So, experience design covers all forms of interaction with products, services and spaces.

Good experience design is interactive, participatory and collaborative. One approach to designing experiences that affect positive change in ethical and equitable ways is to first understand the motivation or social interaction and then design aspects of the experience that have positive cues and rewards to direct engagement.

From here you create environments that enable and enhance the experience, leverage healthy competition or motivators (see gamification below) and then when implemented, help to create the desired change.

Especially when implementing a circular economy solution, one of the major hurdles will be the willingness of customers to accept and adopt the new behaviors required for the circular solution to work. Whether it's returning or repairing something or engaging in a way that is not the current status quo, how you design the experience is critical to your circular solutions success.

GAMIFICATION

Gamification is the use of game mechanics in non-gaming environments, and it's become a hot tool

EXPERIENCE FLOW

DISCOVER	DEFINE	DESIGN	DEPLOY	MEASURE
INTERVIEWS	EXPERIENCES	SKETCHES	MARKUP	CHANGE
MAPS	USER STORIES	WIRE FRAMES	SCRIPTS	METRICS
AUDITS	STORYBOARDS	MOODBOARDS	STYLE SHEETS	ANALYSIS
ANALYSIS	JOURNEY MAPS	GAMES	GRAPHICS	ACCESSIBILITY
SURVEYS	SITE MAPS	CO CREATION	PATTERNS	IMPROVEMENTS
PERSONAS		USABILITY TEST	STYLE GUIDES	
		PROTOTYPES	EXPERIMENTS	

A POSITIVE APPROACH

   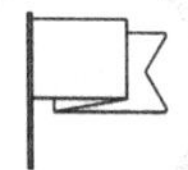 

UNDERSTAND	DESIGN	CREATE	LEVERAGE	USE
MOTIVATION AND SOCIAL BEHAVIOR	POSITIVE AND REWARDING EXPERIENCE	ENVIRONMENTS THAT ALLOW CHANGE TO HAPPEN	HEALTHY COMPETITION	DYNAMIC GAME MECHANICS

for user experience design because it so effectively enhances and motivates engagement in many different contexts (when it's deployed well).

Gamification is a technique of dissecting and exploring the principles that motivate action in a game, then implementing mechanics like this into a product, service, system or environment design. Nearly all apps use gamification principles.

Game mechanics are the things that make you behave or perform when playing a game; given that so many of us are familiar with them, they can easily be implemented in entirely different contexts and still have a positive effect.

As a tool for motivating engagement, gamification is being employed across industries because the human mind responds positively to challenge and reward. Four Ms help design engaging, cognitively-rich experiences using gamification: mechanics, mechanisms, modes and motivators.

MECHANICS: The parts that you include in your design that work together to make it operate in the way you want. These are the things that you decipher and direct from other game play arenas, like when you use a time restriction to get people to run around a room collecting things or when you build in an obstacle. Mechanics are the nuts and bolts of how your gamified experience works.

MECHANISMS: The drivers and influencers of action within the arenas you are creating. These are the things that you include to get people to act, such as having a leaderboard, which works to get players excited and replaying rounds.

MODES: The ways of playing/operating within the system. For example, you might make people walk around a room blindfolded so that they have to experience the space differently or make people respond to a quiz before they can enter.

MOTIVATORS: The things that make the players act or perform in the desired way. These are the rewards that you use to progress play and keep people interested, like when you pass Go, you get $200. This acts as a constant motivator to keep playing, even if you are losing the game. Motivators are the reasons you want to participate.

Gamification is, however, not just about making things "fun" and using play mechanics. It's a much more intricate, refined design process that motivates actions in a given context. It's also a way of making an experience more enjoyable, engaging, memorable and cognitively-rewarding for participants.

COGNITIVE EXPERIENCES

One of the reasons experience design works so well is that it triggers the reward center in the brain (as does gamification).

We love things that are unique, and we often rate pleasurable experiences more highly. The attention to detail in a nice hotel or the beautiful ease that a website experience offers — these impact the mind by evoking emotions and positive feelings that keep us coming back.

Beautifully-designed experiences that support behavior and cultural change are key to enacting sustainable solutions. Many of the new business approaches part of this transition are about building long-term relationships, returning products, having people do their own repairs, etc. This means that companies need to design highly effective, desirable and frictionless experiences that evoke cognitive rewards.

THINGS TO CONSIDER:

- How does your experience evoke a desire to participate?
- Where are the current friction points and how can you design to resolve them?
- Are you accidently excluding some people through your experience design? How can you ensure you create inclusive designs?
- As you implement new types of offerings for the circular economy, what experiences or engagement challenges might you encounter and how can you design the product/offering to work around these?
- What motivators can you build into your approach to increase continual participation?

Also consider that there is a dark side to all of this. Known as dark partnering, this is a technique whereby companies exploit cognitive weaknesses in the human mind and deploy gamification principles in ways that confuse and misdirect people into buying/using something they may not want or need or create addictive patterns (like the fact that continuous scroll on social media mimics the mechanics of a slot machine, creating an addictive reward cycle).

Any of these tools should be used in accordance with a strong ethical framework and be about creating collaborative experiences with your customers and stakeholders, not exploitative or manipulative ones.

DESIGNING EXPERIENCES FOR THE CIRCULAR ECONOMY

Every industry and product category will need a different combination of business and design approaches to deliver their core value within the circular economy.

There is so much scope for innovation in sustainability — doing more with less, cycling materials around the economy, collaborating with adjacent businesses or even direct competitors and working with customers to design highly effective experiences that allow for ongoing relationships and services provisions are all within the realm of possibility.

So much of what we need to create is currently undiscovered; we need to test and iterate the different ways we can deliver value into the economy in ways that eliminate waste and cycle materials around so that we reduce the strain on nature.

Here are some of the main approaches to designing a circular business model:

REUSE: Products are delivered as closed-loop and shared reuse systems; for example, replacing disposable and single-use items such as packaging with managed assets that people borrow and then return for refilling. Often technology is a critical part of the reuse system since assets need to be managed, collected, cleaned and redeployed efficiently.

"Circular business models modify the pattern of product and material flows through the economy."

— OECD Business Model for Circular Economy Report, 2018

EXPERIENCE IMPACT ASSESSMENT TOOL:
HOW TO DO A JOURNEY MAP

MATERIALS NEEDED
Large pieces of paper
Different colored pens and markers

A customer journey map is a way of visually exploring the steps a customer goes through as they interact with your product or service. It's usually used to establish pain points and frustrations a customer may have, or test a new approach to delivering them a service.

You can adapt it to identify ways your customer may be directed or encouraged to engage with new desirable behaviors or practices to support implementing a new approach.

Map all the steps that a customer goes through, identifying the touchpoints and key parts of your service system. Explore where there may be failings or frictions and identify what emotions, benefits or experiences the customer will have at each of the key engagement points.

Start with your current offering, understand the relationships between how a customer is engaging with your business and the impacts of these actions, then you can redesign the experiences, services, and communication to help reduce your service impacts.

Using the example of the bike share depot seen below as a reference, create your own customer journey map starting with the provided template on the next page.

JOURNEY MAP

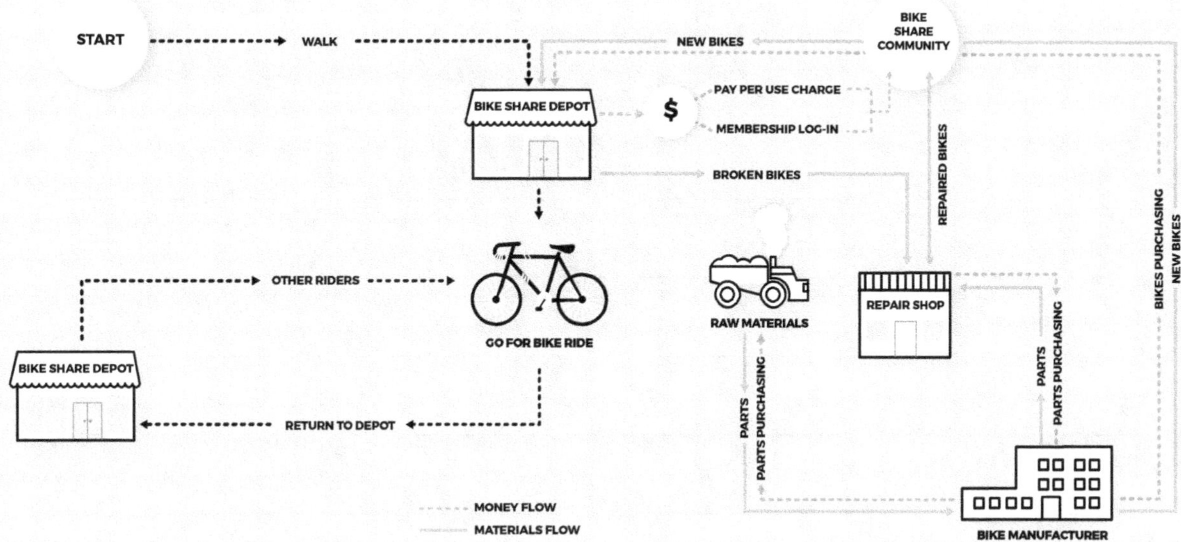

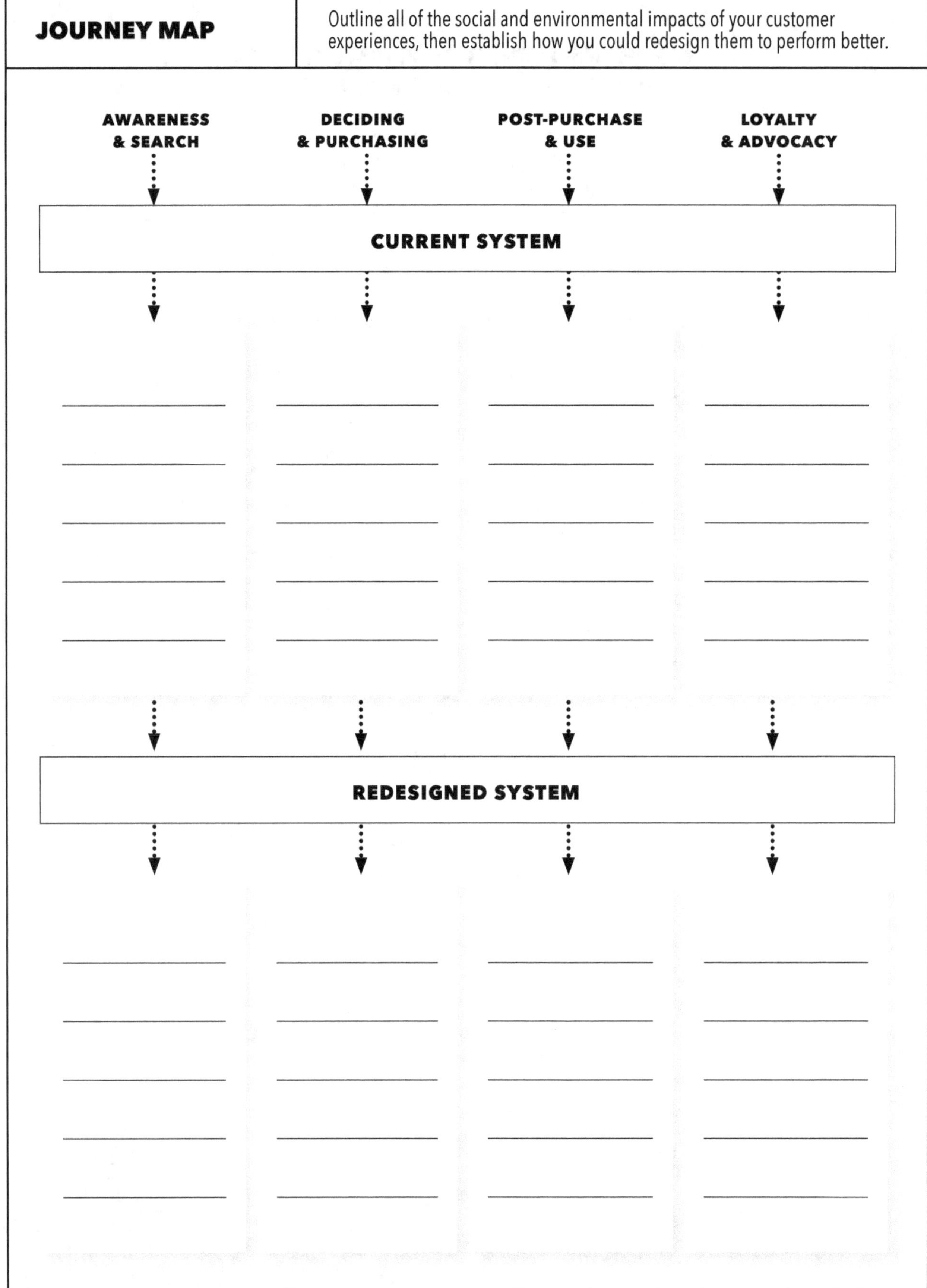

JOURNEY MAP

Outline all of the social and environmental impacts of your customer experiences, then establish how you could redesign them to perform better.

AWARENESS & SEARCH
DECIDING & PURCHASING
POST-PURCHASE & USE
LOYALTY & ADVOCACY

CURRENT SYSTEM

REDESIGNED SYSTEM

REPAIR: Designing products to have extended life spans by providing repair services and maximizing likelihood of repair during use and EOL phases. This includes offering repairs services in store or manuals for others, as well as parts that enable customers to repair/upgrade their items over time.

SUBSCRIPTION: Products are provided as closed-loop systems in which the customer subscribes to receive regular reusable and returnable products as part of a circular system. This is being deployed by food retailers, whereby products such as ice cream and sauces are provided in reusable packaging that the customer returns each time they reorder.

REMANUFACTURE: Creating products within a closed-loop system where they are intended to be taken back, reconditioned or fed back into the production cycle to create new high-value products. This is perfect for technology products. Some suppliers have started designing modular products that they can take apart and redeploy within their own manufacturing system, saving money and resources.

RESELL: The resell of products in the secondhand goods market is actively encouraged by the producer, making it easy to do so and supporting the continuation of functionality by increasing the product's usable life span.

BUYBACK: Producers offer to buy back their products, repair and resell them. This is being rolled out by companies such as Ikea right now. When a producer sees a longer term economic gain from reselling their own items, they are incentivized to design them to last longer.

WASTE AS A RESOURCE: Products are made from the waste of other systems or to ensure that their own byproducts are absorbed into a new system.

CIRCULAR SUPPLIES: Products are part of the supply model, and consumers collaborate to share resources and ensure that circular products are available on the market.

PRODUCT LIFE EXTENSION: Challenging the traditional model of lots of customers buying individual units by offering higher-value, longer-term products and ensuring they are utilized — perhaps with a pay-per-use model or another way of ensuring that materials stay in the economy longer.

RESOURCE RECOVERY: Recovering previously abandoned resources, such as mining landfills or extracting materials from old technology, and getting valuable resources back into the economy to ensure that they are circulated back into the system. Food waste collection services and resell apps are examples of this.

SHARING PLATFORMS: Encouraging the use of platforms and networks to share resources, a classic example of this is the laundromat that enables people to share the use of a service rather than owning their own. There are many examples of fashion rental services that promote sharing as well.

DESIGNING CIRCULAR SOLUTIONS

You know your business best. There may be one or more of these solutions that jumps out at you as being a perfect fit for a new type of business model, or it may be that you need to explore divergent options specific to your industry and business case.

There are limitations to implementing a circular economy, but many of them are cognitive and cultural. So, the best way to get started is to explore which possibilities could work for you. Avoid limiting your potential before you have even started! Road test the possibilities for designing entirely new experiences for your customers and consider what the future of your industry and business will look like when more and more companies adapt to the circular and sustainable economy we are entering into.

THREE SIMPLE STEPS TO GET YOU STARTED

(1) Assess who in your industry is already adopting circular approaches, what has and hasn't worked for them, and learn from this for your system.

(2) Draft a new service offering that employs a circular business model. Test it with stakeholders to gauge their perception and willingness to adopt it, then take this data to feed into the next step.

(3) Explore collaborations and connections with other players that will help you enact a circular business solution; much of the possibility is in the connections!

<table>
<tr><td>

CIRCULAR REDESIGN

</td><td>

Consider the functionality of your product offering and use the circular business approaches and sustainable design considerations to consider ways your offerings can be redesigned to be more circular.

</td></tr>
</table>

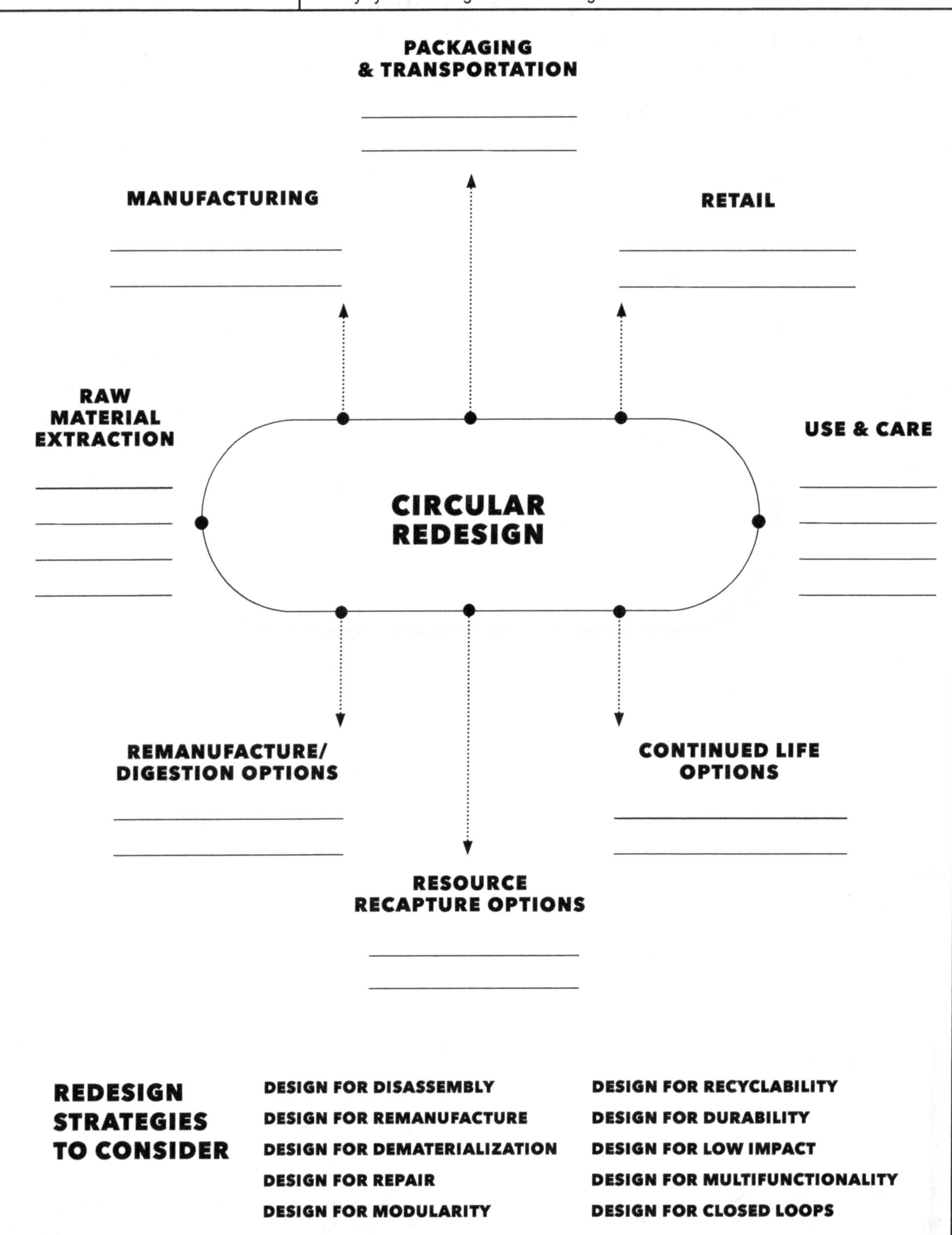

REDESIGN STRATEGIES TO CONSIDER

DESIGN FOR DISASSEMBLY
DESIGN FOR REMANUFACTURE
DESIGN FOR DEMATERIALIZATION
DESIGN FOR REPAIR
DESIGN FOR MODULARITY

DESIGN FOR RECYCLABILITY
DESIGN FOR DURABILITY
DESIGN FOR LOW IMPACT
DESIGN FOR MULTIFUNCTIONALITY
DESIGN FOR CLOSED LOOPS

REFLECTION ACTIVITY

PART 3 RECAP

1 Have impact assessments already been conducted within your organization? If so, how can you connect with the people and teams who are working to document your organization's impacts? If not, what can you do to advocate for the impact assessment process to begin?

2 Considering all 18 areas of impacts, what are the top 3 areas of impact your organization has? How can you begin an initiative to address those impacts?

3 What type of resources and support are needed to activate greater change towards sustainability in your organization?

4 Have you been able to complete a life cycle or supply chain map of your main product offerings? If so, what were your top three takeaways? If not, what needs to happen to ensure that your organization gets one done and assesses those impact areas?

5 Have you conducted a social impact assessment that covers your entire supply chain? If so, what is an area that your organization can begin to improve immediately? If not, what resources or support do you need to make it happen?

6 What circular business models best fit the industry you are in? Have you explored and benchmarked what others are doing to apply circular solutions to their business?

7 What feels exciting to you about improving how customers engage with your experience areas? What feels challenging?

8 How would you rate your organization when it comes to providing green skills development to all employees? Which green skills do you feel are the highest priority to implement (sustainability skills, climate literacy, circular economy action, impact assessment, change action, transition leadership)?

☐ DATE COMPLETED ________________________

EPILOGUE

TAKING ACTION

CONGRATULATIONS!

You're now equipped with many of the tools and approaches needed to get started or advance your full systems business sustainability transformation.

Remember that transformation is a process of continual improvement, building on the things you have done before and embracing the bigger changes that need to occur. This requires commitment to identifying your impacts, developing new standards and adopting significant and progressive actions to reduce and rewrite your impacts entirely.

Below are three simple steps to take to benchmark the data you have developed and transform it into actions that will lead to policies, reporting and iteration.

Taking action using a planned, stepped process will allow you to progress along a pathway to long-lasting positive impacts.
You might be ready for a full systems transformation right now, even better! But if you are just starting out and want to ensure that you get from here to a better place, then be sure to get buy-in, set clear targets and equip the right people with the tools and capacity to enact changes.

And of course, don't get caught social washing or greenwashing; make sure you have the properly skilled people on the task, as well as scientific data that backs up any claims you make.

GOING BEYOND THE OBVIOUS

Sustainability is a journey of constant change. It's about understanding and responding to the systems around you and ensuring that your actions are not negatively affecting the planet and the people in your ecosystem. This requires reflection, exploration and action.

There are many ways you can go beyond the obvious and open up truly transformative change. You might not be ready to start that just yet, but as you progress through the changes you are exploring, you can work toward being a leader in your industry and inspiring change in others; this will build a stronger company in the process.

ACTION PLANNING

In this final section of this guidebook, you should consider aspirational opportunities and aim high for exceptional change within your organization.

It will take time, energy and effort, but the long-term goals will result in a more robust organization that has an ethical, positive workforce offering value back to the wider world and community.
Use the worksheets provided to explore your company's sustainability moonshot opportunities, which are the big aspirations and ambitious goals that go beyond the obvious and set the course for transformative change.

CHECKLISTS AND TAKING ACTION

Once you have conducted your audits and assessments, you should now have a clear understanding of your company's general environmental and social impacts across its operations, products and experiences.

1. **CHECKLISTS AND TAKING ACTION:** Take your audit data and turn it into checklists for change.

2. **POLICY DEVELOPMENT:** Once you have identified your sustainability goals and improvement plan, develop and share ambitious policies that will help you get there.

3. **REPORTING AND IMPROVEMENT:** Share your successes and continuous improvement goals by reporting on your baseline data, changes and next goals.

<table>
<tr><td>ACTION PLANNING</td><td>Create an action plan for aspirational and transformational change within your business.</td></tr>
</table>

PARTNERS & STAKEHOLDERS
WHO HELPS US

ACTIVITIES
WHAT WE DO

RESOURCES
WHAT WE HAVE

DISTRIBUTION CHANNELS
HOW WE INTERACT

BUDGET
WHAT THINGS COST

MISSION
WHY WE DO IT

KEY METRICS & IMPACT
HOW WE MEASURE SUCCESS

BENEFICIARIES
WHO THE VALUE IS PROVIDED TO

EXTERNALITIES
POSSIBLE UNINTENDED SIDE EFFECTS

From the initial data collected, you can set goals, develop policies and checklists for changes and design long-term actions for transformation.

Even though we say full system sustainability is not about checking a box, checklists can be very helpful in setting up new processes and ensuring that key changes are being implemented. Checklists and action planning are about setting up processes that move you from the current status quo to a new state where you can reassess and ensure you have reduced your impacts within the set guidelines.

We recommend action checklists, which can be made for anything that supports you in moving through a process.

Specifically they are useful for dealing with waste issues, reducing energy use or getting staff to change their procurement practices.

Likewise, in the product development process, you can have a clear set of actions to ensure that suppliers are ethical, materials are sustainable and full product outcomes fit into the circular economy.

POLICY DEVELOPMENT

Sustainability policies are an important part of setting your internal agenda and communicating to stakeholders. They work well to align your team in the development of robust and transparent practices. Policies are documents that set out the aims and actions of an organization; they align with legal obligations or internal standards and are signed by a senior manager or CEO to demonstrate the company-wide commitment. Policies should:

- Set a clear commitment that people can rally around
- Offer a pathway to action that they can follow and implement
- Include a timeline for a review process to ensure the set goals and targets are met
- Be externally communicated

Written policies help set standards and provide operational frameworks that ensure everyone in your team is on the same page. But they can also create a minimum standard that reduces people's

creativity and restricts solutions. To overcome this, be aspirational but achievable, and set goals and targets that enable an appropriate transition time. There are several types of sustainability policies you should develop, including:

- Environmental policies (like waste reduction by x amount, plastics elimination in the supply chain, etc.)
- Social inclusion policy
- Gender equity and diversity policy
- Fair work and pay policy
- Climate action policy
- Circular economy action plan
- Sustainability alignment plan
- Sustainable procurement plans
- Good governance and ethics

REPORTING AND GOVERNANCE

The way an organization is governed and the choices made around the public reporting of performance across all categories are critical for the transformation to sustainability in your company.

The Board of Directors and C Suite has incredible power over the behaviors, culture, actions and performance of the entire company, so it's critical for them to see the value of sustainability and report on actions taken to increase performance in-line with corporate responsibility.

When ambitious and clear sustainability goals are set from the boardroom, the organization's DNA will change.

Whatever angle you look at it from, be it from a customer desire or financial risk standpoint, there are many reasons why any company should actively engage with more sustainable and ethical corporate governance approaches.

Critically, measurement and reporting of impacts (especially carbon emissions) are quickly becoming a major player in the financial sector — meaning that credit and investment are being tied to an organization's ability to demonstrate that they have a sustainability charter and are taking action.

<table>
<tr><td>POLICY CHECKLIST</td><td>Consider the functionality of your product and use these sustainable design considerations to think through how it can be redesigned to be more circular.</td></tr>
</table>

ASPECT

CONSIDERATION

ASPECT	CONSIDERATION	
REALISTIC AND ASPIRATIONAL ASSESSMENT OF WHAT ACTIONS YOU HAVE AND ARE WILLING TO IMMEDIATELY TAKE	List all the things you have done regarding energy, water, waste, travel, procurement and general operations. Assign an internal mark or value on how you are currently performing and then assign an aspirational list to get you to a 10 out of 10. Use this as the foundations for your policy.	
SET A DATE FOR REVIEW AND REASSESSMENT	Yearly for more broad policies work well, but there may be some cases where the policy needs to be assessed more frequently, especially when you are newly implementing your strategies. Assign a fair amount of time in the responsible people's calendars in advance to ensure that this is done on time.	
BE OPEN AND TRANSPARENT	Avoid making claims you can't keep and be open about things you know you need to improve on. Companies often get the most pushback when they are seen as misdirecting the public about what they are doing, or having accidentally hypocritical policies. Avoid this by being open and transparent about your goals for improvement.	
ALWAYS BE ASPIRATIONAL IN SOME WAY	Your policy should not just be a blanket commitment to change the world, but it should have some solid aspirational and admirable goals that your team and customers can get behind.	
KEEP IT SIMPLE AND CLEAR	Don't overwhelm people with a 100-page policy on sustainable stapler procurement; instead be clear and concise about what needs to be done and how you are doing it (or working towards doing it) better.	
CO-CREATE RATHER THAN DICTATE	If you get your team or even your public involved in some way with the development of your policies, you are much more likely to have a quicker uptake and buy-in, as people will feel more ownership over what has been produced.	
DO THE RESEARCH	It's easy to assume you already know what you need to know, but there is always scope to learn more. Find inspiring case studies or new technologies that will enable the goals to be met and always do research before taking action to ensure you have the best information to make good decisions.	
AIM FOR BETTER	It's very unlikely that you will be the best when starting out, or even when doing this for a significant amount of time, so always aim to do better in the way you set your policies and communicate them out.	
BE MINDFUL OF ACCIDENTAL GREENWASHING	It can be an accident, but it happens more often than not that statements or decisions are made that are more about marketing benefits as opposed to genuine changes. Do a greenwashing scan on all your creations to ensure you are not accidentally making claims you can't back up or seeking to get some marketing cred instead of doing the work.	
DON'T BE WISHY WASHY	Many policies are generic, overly broad and include words that have no true meaning or actual compliance outcomes. Avoid that at all costs, as you will create something that has no substance and thus does nothing for you.	
BE INSPIRING	How can you ensure that what you are committing to and saying inspires your team and others to comply?	

GOAL SETTING	Work through each of the 18 impact areas and decide on aspirational moonshot goals you will work toward.
OPERATIONAL IMPACT AREAS ENERGY	**OUR MOONSHOT GOAL**
WATER	
INFRASTRUCTURE	
PROCUREMENT	
TRAVEL	
WASTE **PRODUCT IMPACT AREAS** CUSTOMER USE	**OUR MOONSHOT GOAL**
RETAIL	
END OF LIFE	
SUPPLY CHAIN	
MATERIALS	
PACKAGING **EXPERIENTIAL IMPACT AREAS** JOURNEY	**OUR MOONSHOT GOAL**
ENGAGEMENT	
COGNITION	
COMMUNICATION	
SPACE	
DIRECTION	

<table>
<tr><td>

PAST & FUTURE OPPORTUNITIES

</td><td>

Consider the changes and opportunities that exist within your organization, both in the past and the future.

</td></tr>
</table>

PAST CHANGES IN OUR ORGANIZATION & INDUSTRY

STATUS QUO	HOW HAS IT CHANGED?	CHANGE FACTORS & INFLUENCES
__________	__________	__________
__________	__________	__________
__________	__________	__________
__________	__________	__________
__________	__________	__________

FUTURE OPPORTUNITES FOR CHANGE IN OUR ORGANIZATION & INDUSTRY

STATUS QUO	HOW COULD IT CHANGE?	CHANGE FACTORS & INFLUENCES
__________	__________	__________
__________	__________	__________
__________	__________	__________
__________	__________	__________
__________	__________	__________

Sustainability reporting is an organization's practice of publishing information on its economic, environmental and social impacts. There are several reporting frameworks; let's explore some of the main ones.

ENVIRONMENTAL SOCIAL GOVERNANCE (ESG)

ESG defines investment decisions that prioritize the Environmental, Social and Governance factors that are central to measuring the success of a portfolio or performance of a business.

When used as criteria to measure the activity of companies, ESG is supposed to help investors determine the long-term social and environmental benefits, not just the financial aspect of an investment (although there have been some concerns about the types of companies getting ESG ratings and ESG portfolio credibility).

The environmental criteria in ESG includes the company's energy, waste, pollution, natural resource use and animal welfare —many of the operational impacts we have been exploring here. It may also look at the environmental risks that a company is exposed to and assess how they address these, such as issues with ownership of contaminated land, carbon emissions, disposal of hazardous waste, mitigation of toxic emissions or compliance with government environmental regulations.

The social criteria focuses on the company's business and stakeholder relationships, along with how it works with suppliers and treats workers.

The governance criteria looks at how the company uses transparent and appropriate accounting methods to measure and report on performance, as well as ensures there is no corruption. This criteria also explores the avoidance of conflicts of interest and ensures that ethical practices are adhered to by the company's leaders, such as not using political contributions to obtain favorable treatment and not partaking in illegal practices.

In the European Union, there is an ESG taxonomy that sets standards for what can be included in ESG criteria, and now there is a legal requirement for financial and publicly-listed companies to disclose their performance inline with ESG criteria.

ESG questions to consider:

- Does the company provide a high level of worker health and safety?
- How is social impact measured and improved?
- Does the company donate profits to the local community or have an employee volunteer program to give back?
- Does the company measure and reduce environmental impacts?
- Does the company offer solutions that address environmental issues such as climate change?
- Are products and packaging designed to be sustainable and part of the circular economy?
- Does the company have ethical and equitable operating policies?
- Are stakeholders given an opportunity to vote on important issues?

CORPORATE SOCIAL RESPONSIBILITY

Often referred to as CSR, Corporate Social Responsibility is a form of business assessment and self-regulation that seeks to reduce the impacts of activities and contribute to positive goals of ethical conduct, philanthropic activity, environmental stewardship and charitable actions.

The goal is social and environmental accountability whereby companies set their own targets and report annually on their progress.

Over the years CSR reporting has become popular, and there has been much pushback on the lack of transformative change as a result of this type of reporting.

Whilst CSR reporting has provided some wins, many companies cherry-pick what they share publicly to avoid deeper issues.

GLOBAL REPORTING INITIATIVE (GRI)

The Global Reporting Initiative (GRI: www.globalreporting.org) is a global organization that develops standards to support businesses and to encourage governments to understand and communicate their sustainability impacts in a standardized, legitimate way. As mentioned

ESG SELECTION CRITERIA

Not all companies have to meet every one of these, although it would be good if they did. often, the investors seek out companies that align with their own investing values.

ENVIRONMENTAL	SOCIAL	GOVERNANCE
• Climate change • Natural resource use • Energy use • Pollution & waste • General environmental performance • Biodiversity • Product, packaging, material impacts	• Worker health & safety • Ethical employment conditions • Product liability • Volunteering & community investement • Gender & diversity • Human rights	• Corporate transparency • Conflicts of interest • Corruption and tax avoidance • Business ethics • Regulatory compliance • Lobbying

previously, the GRI is the most widely used sustainability reporting framework in the world.

A core goal of the GRI initiative is to encourage and allow organizations to be transparent and accountable by understanding and then disclosing their impacts.

The standards are designed around a universal modular system that ensures a company's sustainability report provides an inclusive picture of their impacts and impact management.

Additional reporting frameworks:

- UN Global Compact
- Carbon Disclosure Project
- The Sustainability Accounting Standards Board (SASB)
- Task Force on Climate-Related Financial Disclosures (TCFD)
- European Sustainability Reporting Standards
- International Sustainability Standards Board
- Integrated Reporting (IR)
- OECD Guidelines for Multinational Enterprises
- European Union's Taxonomy for Sustainable Activities

When developing reports, consider the following:

1. State the company's strategic sustainability goals.
2. Report on your baseline audit data for all impact areas.
3. Provide a status report on how you're improving or plan to do so if it's your first report.
4. Be open and transparent.
5. List the company's sustainability activities for that year or period of reporting.
6. Include dates that the reporting covers.
7. Include a compelling and honest message from the CEO or senior leader.
8. Summarize actions taken and state mid to long-term goals.
9. Address the three tiers of sustainability: social, economic and environmental impacts.
10. Also address worker rights, safety and diversity across your entire supply chain.
11. Be clear about your timeline and trajectory.
12. Don't cherry pick data that makes you look good.

ISSUES WITH SUSTAINABILITY REPORTING

Like anything else, a sustainability report will be as good as the people doing it; it offers a significant scope for accidental or intentional greenwashing. Nearly every big company now does some form of CSR reporting, but that doesn't mean that they are a sustainable company!

Often they don't provide the right context to understand what the larger picture is, and in many cases, data is selected to show only what looks good. This is not a sincere or substance-based approach; misleading people into thinking you have solved all your impact issues will not get you to a better outcome.

MAINTAINING MOMENTUM

Our collective future relies on us figuring out how to meet human needs without destroying the planet. Every single business in the world needs to take action now to ensure that it is a good corporate citizen that knows its impacts and is constantly making better decisions.

The crises we face, from climate change to ocean plastic waste, the sixth great extinction, ecosystem destruction and social inequity — these are all changeable! We can restore and regenerate nature, create a more ethical society and ensure that the things we make are part of a circular economy.

These challenges are opportunities in disguise, just waiting for creative people with foresight and passion to help take action to address them.

Remember, sustainability is a process of transformation with many untapped opportunities just waiting for you to uncover them.

This is just the start; there is so much more to discover and do to ensure that you future-proof

Leadership and courage is crucial to the transformation.

business decisions and develop products and services that treat nature and fellow humans with respect.

Whatever you are at now, just starting out or leading the way, your current position should not be the end of your actions — it's the beginning. The journey to a better future is always ongoing and requires many smart, creative and courageous people.

People like you!

Whilst it can seem overwhelming when the magnitude of the issues are constantly presented as huge problems, remember that every problem holds its own solution, and the only way they will be tackled is by multiple actions working away at solving them.

Companies that don't take significant action today will be left scrambling to catch up in the near future.

The one sector of society that has the most influence (and let's be honest, the most money) to make change is business! Those who are already taking action to address their impacts are seeing the rewards from their leadership.

Start or expand your sustainability conversation in-house today, and know that it's a journey of discovery that will result in greater performance, more integrity and a better future for all of us.

The pathway to this better future is paved with many micro and macro transformation changes.

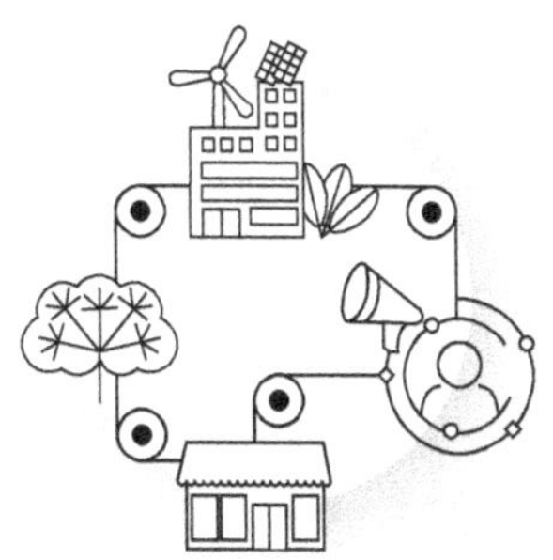

IS SUSTAINABILITY ENOUGH?

Sustainability as a technical toolset and approach to understanding and reducing environmental impacts of actions is as good as the people using it.

All tools can be abused and misused; sustainability is not immune to this. However, the alternative to figuring out how to sustain our species within the means and resources of this beautiful planet is both one of the biggest challenges and opportunities of our time.

The important thing to remember is that we live in a complex, constantly evolving system of which we are a part of and thus we need to be adaptive and responsive to the systems around us. The decisions we make today determine the future we will live in tomorrow, so the more minds that are invested in helping to explore, experiment and design alternatives to the polluting and wasteful status quo, the quicker we will create a better future.

The more people who embrace this with sincerity and integrity, the more likely we are to move into a future that works better than today. The more resistance and misuse, the increased chance we will end up dealing with more disasters of our own making.

The end goal is a restorative and regenerative economy where we meet all human needs in ways that don't destroy and damage the systems that sustain life.

And the first change starts with you.

SUSTAINABILITY SKILLS DEVELOPMENT

In order to fully integrate sustainability into your business DNA, you need all of your team members to be leveled up with the content, resources, concepts and tools to ensure success.

Like any new industry change (think from analog to digital or the rise of e-commerce, etc.), sustainability and the transition to the circular economy are critical skills of the 21st century, so invest in your team.

Ensure your team has access to the best practices and knowledge sets they need to assess and build solutions that will position your company at the forefront of this transformation, rather than trail behind others in your sector who have the foresight to fully embrace this change.

Design your employees' experience as much as you create a frictionless and exciting reason for your customers to engage, and you will attract and retain the best talent, be industry leaders and see the positive innovation opportunities that these changes enable.

NEXT STEPS & PROFESSIONAL DEVELOPMENT

We have three leading platforms for further development of important skills and capacity for activating sustainability:

UNSCHOOL: Providing over 100 courses for professionals wanting to transition to the circular economy and/or apply sustainability and systems thinking to their career, The UnSchool offers a range of courses and certification programs.

We also offer support for your business sustainability development in our online Business Sustainability Subscription Pack or the online 4-Week Sprint on the 3 Dimensions of Sustainability in Business.

SWIVEL SKILLS: Designed for in-house corporate online team training, our certification program for sustainability skills development offers you all that you need to get started.

This highly effective online professional development content is designed to support the rapid uptake of core concepts, tools and approaches to integrating sustainability into decision making and across your business.

DISRUPT DESIGN: Through our design and education agency, we curate experiences, workshops and provocations that support business transformation.

From tailored in-house training to toolkit development, if you want a customized experience, reach out to find out how we can help.

We have an extensive sustainability and circular economy skills training platform available at swivelskills. com. The activities and worksheets included in this guidebook are a great complement to the Swivel Skills organizational training program.

LEARN MORE ABOUT US

Explore commissioned projects and interventions.
DISRUPTDESIGN.CO

Discover more about the UnSchool, our methods and community.
UNSCHOOLS.CO

Engage with B2C online learning, classes, certifications, tools and resources in systems thinking, sustainability sciences and design.
ONLINE.UNSCHOOLS.CO

Access in-house B2B online and hybrid customizable corporate training packages ranging from foundational levels through to advanced training in sustainability for business.
SWIVELSKILLS.COM

WE ARE HERE TO HELP YOU MAKE CHANGE

BIBLIOGRAPHY

Azqueta, D. and Sotelsek, D., 2007. Valuing nature: From environmental impacts to natural capital. Ecological Economics, 63(1), pp.22-30.

Bar-On, Y.M., Phillips, R. and Milo, R., 2018. The biomass distribution on Earth. Proceedings of the National Academy of Sciences, 115(25), pp.6506-6511.

Brundtland, G.H., 1987. Our common future—Call for action. Environmental Conservation, 14(4), pp.291-294.

Benyus, J.M., 2002. Biomimicry: Innovation inspired by nature, Harper Perennial.

Burdge, R.J. and Vanclay, F., 2009. Social impact assessment, Csiro Publishing.

Caradonna, J.L., 2014. Sustainability: A history. Oxford University Press.

Cavicchioli, R., Ripple, W.J., Timmis, K.N. et al. Scientists' warning to humanity: microorganisms and climate change. Nat Rev Microbiol 17, 569–586 (2019).

Crutzen, P.J., 2006. The "anthropocene". In Earth system science in the anthropocene (pp. 13-18). Springer, Berlin, Heidelberg.

Dawkins, R. 1976, The Selfish Gene, Oxford University Press.

de Wit, M. 2021, Circular Gap Report 2021, The Platform for Accelerating the Circular Economy, accessed, Aug 2022: https://www.circle-economy.com/resources/circularity-gap-report-2021

de Wit, M. 2020, Circularity Gap Report 2020, The Platform for Accelerating the Circular Economy, available online https://www.circularity-gap.world

Duhigg, C., 2012. The power of habit: Why we do what we do in life and business (Vol. 34, No. 10). Random House.

Dunning, D., 2011. The Dunning–Kruger effect: On being ignorant of one's own ignorance. In Advances in experimental social psychology (Vol. 44, pp. 247-296). Academic Press.

Fuller, R., Landrigan, P.J., Balakrishnan, K., Bathan, G., Bose-O'Reilly, S., Brauer, M., Caravanos, J., Chiles, T., Cohen, A., Corra, L. and Cropper, M., 2022. Pollution and health: a progress update. The Lancet Planetary Health.

Gillespie, T.R., Jones, K.E., Dobson, A.P., Clennon, J.A. and Pascual, M., 2021. COVID⊠Clarity demands unification of health and environmental policy. Global Change Biology, 27(7), pp.1319-1321.

Giddens, A., 1984. Elements of the theory of structuration. Published In, Practicing History: New Directions in Historical Writing After the Linguistic Turn, Routledge, 2004.

Gössling, S., Araña, J.E. and Aguiar-Quintana, J.T., 2019. Towel reuse in hotels: Importance of normative appeal designs. Tourism Management, 70, pp.273-283

Helm, D., 2015. Natural capital: valuing the planet. Yale University Press.

Hein, L., Bagstad, K.J., Obst, C., Edens, B., Schenau, S., Castillo, G., Soulard, F., Brown, C., Driver, A., Bordt, M. and Steurer, A., 2020. Progress in natural capital accounting for ecosystems. Science, 367(6477), pp.514-515.

Kaza, S., Yao, L., Bhada-Tata, P. and Van Woerden, F., 2018. What a waste 2.0: a global snapshot of solid waste management to 2050. World Bank Publications.

Kübler-Ross, E., 1997. The wheel of life. Simon and Schuster.

Lakoff, G., 2004. Don't think of an elephant: Progressive values and the framing wars—a progressive guide to action. White River Junction, VT: Chelsea Green Publishing.

Lakoff, G., 2010. Why it matters how we frame the environment. Environmental communication, 4(1), pp.70-81.

Lewin, K., 1946. Force field analysis. The 1973 annual handbook for group facilitators, 111, p.13.

Lovelock, J., 2003. Gaia: the living Earth. Nature, 426(6968), pp.769-770.

Meadows, D.H., 2008. Thinking in systems: A primer. Chelsea Green Publishing.

Molotoks, A., Smith, P. and Dawson, T.P., 2021. Impacts of land use, population, and climate change on global food security. Food and Energy Security, 10(1), p.e261.

Mora, C., Tittensor, D.P., Adl, S., Simpson, A.G. and Worm, B., 2011. How many species are there on Earth and in the ocean?. PLoS biology, 9(8), p.e1001127.

Natural Capital Partners, Reality Check: Climate Action and Commitments of the Fortune Global 500, Published September 21, 2021, accessed online, Sept, 21: https://www.naturalcapitalpartners.com/insights/reality-check

Nisbet, M.C., 2009. Communicating climate change: Why frames matter for public engagement. Environment: Science and policy for sustainable development, 51(2), pp.12-23.

Oberle, B., Bringezu, S., Hatfield-Dodds, S., Hellweg, S., Schandl, H., Clement, J., Cabernard, L., Che, N., Chen, D., Droz-Georget, H. and Ekins, P., 2019. Global resources outlook 2019: natural resources for the future we want.

OECD, 2022, Global Plastics Outlook, available online: https://www.oecd-ilibrary.org/environment/global-plastics-outlook_de747aef-en

Raworth, K., 2017. Doughnut economics: seven ways to think like a 21st-century economist. Chelsea Green Publishing.

Rockström, J., Steffen, W., Noone, K., Persson, Å., Chapin III, F.S., Lambin, E., Lenton, T.M., Scheffer, M., Folke, C., Schellnhuber, H.J. and Nykvist, B., 2009. Planetary boundaries: exploring the safe operating space for humanity. Ecology and society, 14(2).

Stahel, W.R., 2016. The circular economy. Nature, 531(7595), pp.435-438.

Wackernagel, M. and Rees, W., 1998. Our ecological footprint: reducing human impact on the earth (Vol. 9). New society publishers.

Schumann, C. (2018). Is Topic Fatigue an International Problem? Four Theses . Global Media Journal - German Edition, 8(2). Retrieved from: https://www.globalmediajournal.de/index.php/gmj/article/view/25

Steffen, W., Broadgate, W., Deutsch, L., Gaffney, O. and Ludwig, C., 2015. The trajectory of the Anthropocene: the great acceleration. The Anthropocene Review, 2(1), pp.81-98.

Schumacher, E.F., 1973. Small is beautiful: economics as if people mattered. London: Blond & Briggs.

Wackernagel, M. and Rees, W., 1998. Our ecological footprint: reducing human impact on the earth (Vol. 9). New society publishers.

WEF: World Economic Forum, 2019, A New Circular Vision for Electronics Time for a Global Reboot, available online: https://www.weforum.org/reports/a-new-circular-vision-for-electronics-time-for-a-global-reboot

World Bank, 2020, Global Public Procurement Database: Share, Compare, Improve!, available online: https://www.worldbank.org/en/news/feature/2020/03/23/global-public-procurement-database-share-compare-improve